Praise for the Book

When you are just starting out in your career, the prospect of finding your way towards a lofty goal can seem so daunting, especially if you don't have people in your family who have navigated the corporate paths. It can very much be a snakes and ladders career path! Now thanks to Mary-Beth, you don't have to make the slides down, and find the energy for the ladder climbs as some of us have! This is a great guide for those looking for help on how to make big bold career moves and encourages the reader to draw upon their unique backgrounds to differentiate themselves and draw upon transferable lessons.

Dr Jen Frahm
Co-Founder Agile Change Leadership Institute

There is no better time than the present, to step into a future that excites your soul and reveals your true potential. For years to come you will thank yourself for believing in your true value and there is no better feeling. The first step is big, bold, and brave. And then comes an excitement that builds its own momentum. As a woman who raised five children including two sets of twins while juggling three degrees on her long and windy road to C-Suite, this is the book I wish I had 25 years ago!

Beautifully written, highly engaging, and extremely practical, it's what every woman needs to read on their unique journey of becoming. No longer will you hesitate in trusting your knowledge, skills and expertise. It's your time to confidently tread a new path, well equipped by the framework provided to guide your future success.

Annie Gibbins
Founder and CEO Women's Biz Global

Most of us, will at some time, move from one role to another, from one career to another. When that time comes, are you prepared to be the best you can be? Mary-Beth provides great insights and advice from her experience as the singer who became a CIO.

Will you know the value you will bring to the new role or career? Will you capture all the transferrable skills you can bring from past positions? What will you do when you start to doubt yourself? What will you do if you do not get the role and most importantly what will you learn?

Mary-Beth provides you with the answers in this beautifully written autobiographical narrative.

Karen Ferris
Change Management Rebel with a Cause

Mary-Beth's focus on helping people to transition in their careers is an increasingly essential skill to learn in a modern, technology driven, fast paced world. Her ability to tell stories that engage means that the lessons in career and leadership are accessible to anyone.

I especially love how she has been able to turn her expertise in change management to help the individual navigate through change in their career.

Buy a copy today, read it and stop hesitating about making changes in your career. Even better, buy a second copy and give it to someone who needs encouragement to reach their own destiny.

Amanda Blesing
C-suite Mentor, CEO & Founder, The She-Suite® Club

When now, means NOW!
A handbook for career change, advancement and progression

WHEN NOW, MEANS NOW!

A handbook for career change, advancement and progression

MARY-BETH HOSKING

First published in 2023 by Quantum Transformation | Melbourne

ISBN: 978-0-6489006-2-7 (pbk)

eISBN: 978-0-6489006-3-4 (ebook)

A catalogue record for this book is available from the National Library of Australia

Typeset, printed and bound in Australia by BookPOD

NATIONAL LIBRARY OF AUSTRALIA

A catalogue record for this book is available from the National Library of Australia

Contents

To my wonderful and loving husband Stuart,
who has never made me feel less than, you always
said "you do you" well here I am "doing me".

To my high school bestie Bee Lin,
for all those auditions you sat through.

To my father, I get it now.

When I was fifteen, all I wanted to do was sing.

It was all I wanted, until the day that it wasn't.

Then I had a decision to make.

Foreword

I first met Mary-Beth Hosking at a business introduction meeting. I was immediately drawn to her. Not only because we instantly recognised that we shared a passion – writing –but also because of Mary-Beth herself. She has a curiosity, openness and compassion that only the very best leaders display.

Mary-Beth is an expert on creating a career that matters, but the way she does it is unique. Her focus is on two strong pillars that underpin all her decisions: legacy, and joy. Legacy is something she first learned at her father's funeral. Until then, she'd thought of her dad as a talented and dedicated musician, a hard-working father of five daughters. But she also discovered just how many of his colleagues credited him with their own success. He was someone who found ways to train, upskill, and promote his people. To Mary-Beth, that's true leadership. That's how you have longevity in any work you do.

Joy is something Mary-Beth learned during her first career. Performing at gigs that lasted four or even six hours straight, she experienced firsthand the joy of meaningful work, and also, the struggle of it. She learned about feedback – how to receive it and how to give it – in the sometimes very uncontrolled environment of a live audience. She learned fast that in a stressful situation, she's the person thinking, 'How do I solve my way out of this?'

What impresses me most about Mary-Beth is how committed she is to her people. When her very first team wasn't performing well, Mary-Beth didn't write it off as 'a bad team', she decided they weren't performing because she wasn't performing. And she decided to do better. So, she completed a Masters of Business & Technology specifically so she could be a better leader. To this day, she continues to study leadership so she can improve and expand her skills.

Mary-Beth wants her legacy to be found in the next tier of leaders, and the tier after that. She believes that the measure of success for her, as a leader, is whether or not everyone in her team is having the most amazing careers they can have.

I asked Mary-Beth what advice she'd give the twenty-something her, and she said: grab every opportunity with both hands, and enjoy the ride.

I hope you'll grab this book with both hands.

And enjoy the ride!

Katrina Macdermid
Creator of Humanising IT™

Who am I?

My name is Mary-Beth Hosking and I am an IT leader living and working in Australia. I guess the first question you might be asking is how am I qualified to be writing about career change, advancement and progression? Great question!

Let me begin with my journey.

When I was six years old, I was diagnosed with a particularly extreme form of psoriasis. For anyone not familiar with this rather unpleasant skin condition it generally forms thick scaly patches of skin on your elbows and knees – for me it was over 95% of my body.

This meant that for most of my youth I was hospitalised. This was not an unpleasant time but it meant that I formed some of my strongest friendships with other children whilst in hospital. Most of my friends were afflicted with terminal illnesses and this had a profound effect on me.

Each year as I would return once again for another hospital stay, I would be informed of the passing of yet another friend. This made me extremely sad, as I was confronted with the human condition and mortality, year after year.

Having this childhood experience helped to form my personal purpose and my reason for being; something that many adults still seek to find. For me I felt an intense obligation to live my life as fully as possible for those friends that would not get the chance.

This built an intense level of resiliency within me and a passion to experience as many new things as possible. This passion ignited my curiosity and my need to make a difference and add value in whatever I set my mind to.

I have lived my life with the same passion and energy and fill every day with a sense of gratitude and wonder, and I do this for those who didn't get the chance. I wanted to make the biggest impact possible and this has driven every decision I have made, from my early teens up to now.

How could I have the greatest impact and make the biggest difference in my life? The only way I could see this when I was young was to make a firm decision about my future.

So, why do I feel qualified to write this book and why should you read it?

Throughout my life I have learned how to develop resilience through adversity; I've pivoted my career from singing to IT with plenty in between; I've lead teams and broken through a few glass ceilings, with the cuts and bruises to show for it.

I'm still on this journey, making mistakes, course correcting, planning and searching for joy along the way. I want to share with you what I've learned so far, with the hope that these lessons will help you as well, wherever you are in your career journey.

Know Your Purpose

My father was a classically trained musician who pivoted to jazz and played in a big band every weekend. At the age of fifteen I made the decision to follow in his footsteps and become a performer; I wasn't trained, but I knew I could sing and I decided that this would be my way of honouring my childhood friends, lost along the way.

Thankfully I had sensible parents who insisted I continue my studies, whilst also allowing me to follow my musical passions in my spare time. I would like to say that I studied hard and was a diligent student but the simple truth is, I was not. I didn't want to study hard; I wanted to sing and perform. I could not see any sense in staying in school if I

I was adamant that I was going to be a performer and no one was going to dissuade me.

was going to be a singer. I was adamant that I was going to be a performer and no one was going to dissuade me.

My father was quite perturbed by this. He was an exceptionally talented working musician and spent many years playing every weekend; however, he was an engineer during the day, something I conveniently overlooked in my adolescent years. On one of the many occasions of me trying to explain how much I wanted to be a singer, he gave me some wonderful advice, which at the time didn't resonate at all:

> *"Sometimes the timing isn't right and it doesn't matter how much you want it, or how good you are, sometimes it just doesn't happen. If you can find joy in the work you do, weave in aspects of your passion, then if it doesn't happen, it's ok".*

In my teenage brain I knew that I wanted to perform more than anything else, and that this driving desire would somehow make it happen.

At the time I didn't understand what my father meant by "weave in your passion" but as an adult who has pivoted her career and built something extraordinary, I understand him now. Know what brings you joy and it will make your life joyous.

My purpose at this time was very clear: I wanted to experience as much as possible, I wanted to entertain people, and I wanted to do the things that my hospital friends would never be able to do. However, my purpose was muddied and I didn't have clear goals to achieve success.

Choosing the right path

It turns out, you can do something for a long time without having a clear path or goals! I worked for many years trying to break in to the "big time", and I learnt so much along the way. But I was no longer feeling the passion and curiosity that I had thrived on at the start of my performing career, and eventually I made the heartbreaking decision to stop singing and focus on a different path.

The one thing I had firmly locked into my mind was my purpose. Live, learn and experience as much as possible, bring joy to others and do things that my hospital friends could not. Knowing this made the choices I would undertake on my new journey very broad. I also needed to be clear about what I was not prepared to do.

I remained open to different options and began building a catalogue of likes and dislikes. This helped to build a

> *I remained open to different options and began building a catalogue of likes and dislikes.*

framework for me to start choosing the organisations and the type of work I wanted to do, where I could learn more, add value and grow. I knew I'd need to think differently in order to succeed on this new career path.

Be open to the new

For me, I began my corporate role as a temp. If you are unfamiliar with the concept of temping it is similar to short term contract work. In the temping space you are contracted for very short terms, such as one to two weeks. This had a twofold purpose. It was to get me into the world I coveted and to work out where exactly I wanted to be in that world. Temping enabled me to try different industries in rapid succession and to make more discerning decisions about where I wanted to go in the future.

The reality in the temping world is that if you didn't like an industry or a role, you were only in it for a short time. This gave me significant freedom to pick and choose and it also enabled me to move around multiple industries. I worked in finance, IT, logistics, fast moving consumer goods (FMCG), wholesale, retail, marketing, you name it I worked in it until one day I found my place.

I have taken a similar approach to new roles as I did early on in my career. If I am interested in something new, I seek out an opportunity that will avail this to me. I have

For every setback, I've tried to learn and grow from it as much as possible.

always remained open in my thinking and curious as to the next step. For every setback, I've tried to learn and grow from it as much as possible. I have remained resilient because I simply have no choice. My purpose for being does not allow me to stop learning and experiencing and to get back up when knocked down.

I recall my mother saying to me (before I married and changed my surname) that "Cataldo women steer the ship". We are the ones at the helm, ensuring the passengers under our care get to their destination. For me this couldn't be truer. Every team member that has been on the journey with me knows this.

Even now that I have reached the C-Suite I am looking at what makes my role interesting, how I can bring joy to it and how can I learn more from it. I look for the opportunities it may provide and how I will become a better leader from it. Being open to new experiences will always lead to new opportunities and in places you may never have thought. The only way to know how you are tracking is to keep acknowledging what you have learnt and how joyous the role has been for you.

Being open to new experiences will always lead to new opportunities and in places you may never have thought.

Remember where you came from and what it took to get there. Do not discount anything on your journey because it is yours and you should be proud of it.

Key Takeaways:

- *Passion without purpose is not enough.*

- *Become an expert observer of yourself.*

- *Reflect on the joy in each role and use this as your benchmark for success.*

- *Do not discount anything on your journey.*

- *Don't be afraid to pivot, be afraid not to!*

Don't Forget to Plan

When I was singing, I didn't have a plan. I just thought I would sing and a record producer or manager would hear me and then my career would take off. What I now realize is that behind every great performer is someone who had a plan and executed on it.

Every opportunity that availed itself to me was squandered because I did not have a plan or a way to recognize every opportunity to its fullest. I thought I was making my way, when in fact I was just moving from one gig to another, on an endless treadmill, never achieving my goals. Now don't get me wrong, I was making a living but it was not the living I wanted. I was ambitious and I wanted more.

When things didn't happen how I had envisaged, I

It is not enough to just want something to happen, you have to truly think about what you want and put the plan in motion to achieve it.

realized that something was missing. It is not enough to just want something to happen, you have to truly think about what you want and put the plan in motion to achieve it.

The one major life event I was not expecting during this time was the very sudden and unexpected loss of my father. Bereavement isn't really something that you can plan for and when it happens suddenly it can derail you, especially if you do not have a life or career plan. Losing my father was the one thing that impacted me more than I realized at the time and was the catalyst in my decision to change my career path.

If I had had a career or life plan, perhaps I wouldn't have felt so lost and directionless after losing my father. I could have paused what I was doing, but resumed once I felt ready. But I had nothing definite to resume or go back to.

This loss did make me reflect on my career however, and what I wanted. It made me think about my personal values, what was important to me and what I wanted to be known for.

For me it has always been about being successful but more importantly helping others be more successful and I figured that having spent more than 10 years trying to make my mark as a singer perhaps my energies could be better served elsewhere.

Wanting to transition from one career path to another, I really did have to plan this out. It was not going to be enough to want to move from performing to a role in the corporate world. I needed a plan of attack and I was going to have to prove my value in this new world.

I needed a plan of attack and I was going to have to prove my value in this new world.

To do this I would need a plan!

A buffet of choice

In order to plan anything, you need to know exactly where you intend to end up. This can be hard when you're only thinking of the next step. Many times, I have had mentors encourage me to think two roles ahead – but this is hard!

There are many techniques that can be used to help with this decision –making, from a personal SWOT analysis to brain storming or mind mapping sessions. All of these are useful tools, however for me it was about reflecting on my career which helped the most. It showed me those things I really enjoyed and what I wanted to experience more from.

> *Knowing what brings you joy is the first step in your plan to pivot.*

Knowing what brings you joy is the first step in your plan to pivot. A large part of this plan will be underpinning qualifications and work experience that you may need to start on the pathway to your chosen career. For me it was the shift from performance arts to the corporate sector.

I like to think about my career choices like a buffet restaurant. You know the ones, like in Las Vegas, all you can eat, so many choices you sometimes don't know where to begin. I recall going to the MGM Grand and to their Kings Buffet. There was so much selection that I remember standing in the middle of buffet in awe at the sheer amount of choice.

Where do you start when everything looks so tantalising and delicious?

My view of career choice is reasonably simple. When you start out in your career, you may have your secondary school diploma. If you were eating at a buffet that required a qualification to access different areas within then this certificate may allow you access to the soup and salad. If you are

Where do you start when everything looks so tantalising and delicious?

satisfied with the soup and salad then you have achieved what you sought, however if you want something more, such as the carvery, then perhaps you need further skills, qualifications or experience.

With a formal qualification, such as an undergraduate degree, perhaps this opens up the carvery to you. Now you can enjoy the soup and salad and the carvery as well. Then there is the seafood bar, the dessert bar and so on. The more you upskill with formal knowledge and practical application, the more access you have to your career buffet and can consume all you want.

For me when I was starting out on my journey into the corporate world, I knew I had transferable skills and knew what would bring me joy in the workplace. Now I needed to put the plan in place.

Planning based on value

The planning was the more challenging piece, not having really done this in the past. I decided to tackle the planning of my next career step by looking at least ten years ahead. What did my vision of the perfect corporate work life look like?

> *To help me I leant on the career experience within my friendship circle.*

To help me I leant on the career experience within my friendship circle. Most of my friends were in the corporate arena already and this gave me a view of the things I would need to consider as I made my pivot.

In all good plans you need to have some key things including:

1. The outcome you want to achieve

2. The key milestones

3. The tasks to get there

It all seems so simple now, but back then it felt insurmountable. It was at this point that I started to keep my journal. As a budding singer/songwriter I would write ideas and song lyrics all the time. How could I use this same technique to help me on my path? I would start noting my plans and my progress.

As with any good project I kept track of my progress, every task achieved, every milestone checked off. The key thing I learnt during this process has been one thing that I take with me on every new role, the power of **course correction**.

Although I had a view of the outcome I wanted to achieve, it was always a little vague in the beginning. As I made my way towards the outcome it would come into focus and become real and not just a fanciful idea. More often than not the original outcome would evolve into something quite different from the original thought by means of correcting the tasks I was working on; the course would slowly shift to the outcome I now wanted.

A part of this journal began the framework of my Role and Goal analysis. I needed to understand my value, my non-negotiables and my skills gaps and so much more. This concept helped me put together this analysis. To complete this I would spend my time really thinking about what was really important to me.

If you want to use this framework you will need to dig down deep. The further you go, the more enriching the outcome and the more options will present themselves.

Role and goals - an analysis

In this next section I will walk you through what is needed to complete the template which can be found in the appendix. Let's begin:

What do you enjoy about the roles you've had?	How do you want to add value and what adds value for you?
Which companies interest you to work with and why?	What roles interest you to undertake and why?

1 —————————————— 10   L ——————————————
Risk appetite $$ appetite

What are your non-negotiables in a company?	What are you non-negotiables in a role?
Where do you see your skills gaps?	**How will you fill the skills gaps?**

$$H$$

$$1 \qquad\qquad 10$$

$$ appetite   Fulfilment appetite

What did you score for your risk appetite?	What did you score for your $$ appetite?
1-4 means you have a low risk appetite	1-4 means you have a low $$ appetite
5-7 means you have a moderate risk appetite	5-7 means you have a moderate $$ appetite
8-10 means you have a high risk appetite	8-10 means you have a high $$ appetite

What did you score for your fulfillment appetite?	Analysis
1-4 means you have a low fulfilment appetite 5-7 means you have a moderate fulfilment appetite 8-10 means you have a high fulfilment appetite	If you scored low on the risk scale, moderately on the $$ scale and high on the fulfilment scale this shows that you prefer to work in a role that makes you very happy, is a full time secure position that pays within the mid-range bench mark. If you scored high on the risk scale, high on the $$ scale and low on the fulfilment scale this shows that you prefer to work in a role that has the potential to make a high salary, you are prepared to work hard for little fulfilment other than financial and are prepared to take risks.

Section 1: Values

In this section we will look at your personal value statements. This is just for you and you alone. Invest the time and really think about this, it is important if you are thinking about a career change.

SECTION 1: VALUES	
What do you enjoy about the roles you've held?	How do you want to add value and what adds value for you?

SECTION 1: VALUES

What are your non-negotiables in a company?	What are your non- negotiables in a role?

In this section we are focusing on what you have enjoyed about your roles to date. Note down anything that you enjoyed about the roles you have held in the past. Really dig down and think; don't be superficial in your responses. Be as specific as you can.

> An example could be: I enjoy working in a collaborative environment where I am challenged to problem solve complex problems. The reason I like this is because it gives me a sense of pride in accomplishing a challenging task.

Think about the value you add and what adds value for you. Again, you will need to be specific. Adding value for you will be a key differentiator going forward in your career, therefore having an understanding of this will help you find the best organisations for your time investment.

> An example value you add could be: I want to reduce costs within an organisation and see them thrive in economic down-turns. This is important to me because I want to see any organisation I work in, thrive and grow. I have transferable skills in this area and want to continue to show my value in this space.

An example of what adds value for you could be: I have an insatiable appetite for learning and I want to work somewhere that provides learning opportunities to all its employees regardless of their level or position.

Now focus on your non-negotiables. I believe that you have to know what you are not prepared to do to allow other opportunities to open up. Think about the companies you are not prepared to work for and why? Note these here. When you have done this start to think about the roles you are not prepared to do and why. Note these down.

An example of roles you may not want to undertake could be: I have worked in a services industry and this did not resonate for me, therefore I will work in other industries going forward. In order to find joy in my next role it needs to be somewhere that challenges me and somewhere that I really want to work.

An example of organisations may be: I am not prepared to work in an industry that does not meet my personal values. I need to know I am making a difference and it needs to be in a company with a vision and values I can get on board with.

Section 2: Where to from here?

Now that you have worked out what is important to you including your personal values and non-negotiables, it is time to think about "the where".

SECTION 2: WHERE TO FROM HERE	
Which companies interest you to work with and why?	What roles interest you to undertake and why?

1   10   L

Risk appetite $$ appetite

SECTION 2: WHERE TO FROM HERE

Where do you see your skills gaps?	How will you fill the skills gaps?

H

$$ appetite

1   10

Fulfilment appetite

Now think about the companies that really interest you as they may be your next move. Really think about why you want to work there and what you can learn. Think about the roles that you haven't done or would love to do again and note these down. It may be a short list or a long list. Do some research and make sure you are really considering all options.

Next, start to think about skills gaps and where/how you will fill the gaps.

An example could be: I have only worked with small teams and need exposure to more complex working environments. To fill this gap, I will look at opportunities to work on more complex problems or I will look to volunteer in an organization that may fill this gap.

Once this is done let's take a look at your risk, dollar and fulfilment appetite. These are on a scale of zero to 10.

Where do you see yourself on the risk scale? The higher the number the higher the risks you are prepared to take.

Where do you see yourself on the dollar appetite scale? The lower the number, the less you wish to earn; the higher the number, the more you want to earn.

Finally, the fulfilment scale. The higher the number, the more you value fulfilment in a role.

Each of these scales will provide greater insight into the types of roles that will be available for you. What I have found over the years is that each time I sit down to do this analysis (and yes, I do this regularly) the scales, roles and options change. This is true as we grow and mature in roles, and as our careers progress, the things we want when we are younger may change as we get older. This is all part of the journey and it is important to revisit our thinking to ensure we are still on the right path for ourselves.

> *As we grow and mature in roles, and as our careers progress, the things we want when we are younger may change as we get older.*

Section 3: Analysis

In this section we look at the scores and how they reflect on the possible roles that may be available to you.

Looking at the analysis from your risk, dollar and fulfilment perspective, really helps in understanding the next and subsequent moves in your career progression.

SECTION 3: ANALYSIS

What did you score for your Risk Appetite?	What did you score for your $$ Appetite?
1 ———————— 10	L ———————— H
Risk appetite	$$ appetite
1-4 means you have a low risk appetite	1-4 means you have a low $$ appetite
5-7 means you have a moderate risk appetite	5-7 means you have a moderate $$ appetite
8-10 means you have a high risk appetite	8-10 means you have a high $$ appetite

SECTION 3: ANALYSIS

What did you score for your Fulfilment Appetite?	Analysis
1 ———————————— **10** **Fulfilment appetite** 1-4 means you have a low fulfilment appetite 5-7 means you have a moderate fulfilment appetite 8-10 means you have a high fulfilment appetite	If you scored low on the risk scale, moderately on the $$ scale and high on the fulfilment scale this shows that you prefer to work in a role that makes you very happy, is a full time secure position that pays within the mid-range bench mark. If you scored high on the risk scale, high on the $$ scale and low on the fulfilment scale this shows that you prefer to work in a role that has the potential to make a high salary, you are prepared to work hard for little fulfilment other than financial and are prepared to take risks.

Examples of how to read the outcomes:

- If you scored low on the risk scale, moderately on the dollar scale and high on the fulfilment scale this shows that you prefer to work in a role that provides you with a sense of fulfillment, that you know you are doing a great job and enjoying it. The role is secure and pays within a bench mark you are contented with.

- If you scored high on the risk scale, high on the dollar scale and low on the fulfilment scale this shows that you prefer to work in a role that has the potential to make a high salary, you are prepared to work longer hours for lower fulfilment other than financial and are prepared to take risks.

Understanding this will really help you target your next role.

For example, if you are like the second example, you would be well suited to consulting work. There is a lot of pressure and this can sometimes impact your work/ life balance but if fulfilment is on the low side and dollars is on the high side then this may be something that would interest you.

This analysis will also guide you when looking for the next role on social media or online job boards. Knowing how much you need/want to be paid and what balance you seek can be understood from the roles you look at and the outcomes of the interview process.

Signpost the plan

Once the Role and Goal analysis is complete, add these actions to your plan. Each key milestone will be a signpost to keep an eye out for and will help you make your way.

1. Plan out your learning strategy to fill the gaps you have noted

2. Make a list of the companies and roles in which you are interested

3. Research the companies to understand the culture

Like any good plan, sometimes the course may not lead to the desired outcome in the first instance and you must adjust the trajectory slightly to correct the course to the required destination.

4. Link with people in those companies and gain a better understanding of the culture to know if this is really where you want to work

5. Research employment sites to understand current vacancies and what you have that is transferable and where the gaps may be against actual roles

6. Update your social media profiles and resumé to address the requirements of these roles

7. Start applying

Like any good plan, sometimes the course may not lead to the desired outcome in the first instance and you must adjust the trajectory slightly to correct the course to the required destination.

I found myself doing this multiple times and still do this in my career today. It is not a failure to modify the direction you are travelling, it just means that you're taking a different route, and you'll build up transferable skills regardless. Having a

Having a view of what you are seeking helps you create a map to your chosen career path.

view of what you are seeking helps you create a map to your chosen career path.

> 📝 **Key Takeaways:**
>
> - *Your career should be "all you can eat"; try as much as you can and enjoy every morsal.*
>
> - *Don't let your career happen to you, take control now. Take the next steps in your plan.*
>
> - *Course correction is vital in having the career of your choice.*
>
> - *Like Jazz, there are no mistakes only choices, understand the musical guidelines but play outside of these when the mood takes you.*

.

Transferable Skills

When I was fifteen, I had the opportunity to audition for the South Australian Youth Opera. I knew that singing was my destiny, and I wanted nothing more than to make my musician father proud.

I had always thought that my father should have made his life about music but the reality was he had a large family to support. He was my musical hero. Everything I learnt about music was from him.

I remember asking him if he regretted not giving up his family for his music. He thought this was a curious question from his youngest daughter. He said that his greatest achievement were his five daughters. He loved music, always, but his family meant more than anything to him.

As an impetuous teenager, I didn't understand this answer. How could anything be better than music? I eventually grew to understand his response. He found passion in his family and built his life around it. Music afforded us some small luxuries but in the end for him, it was a means to an end.

However, for me, I had my chance. This audition was my first step into a world I knew I was destined for. I practiced, and practiced, until my family and friends couldn't stand it, and then I practiced more. I would sing in front of the bathroom mirror, in front of the family cats, in the backyard, in the front yard. Anywhere that would give me a different sound. I had to be perfect, I had to win this audition. This audition was going to be my avenue out of the little country town I grew up in and would propel me to the stardom I eagerly craved.

The song I chose was "Honeybun" from South Pacific. I sang it hundreds of times until I knew every nuance. I practiced my dance moves to go with the song until I was more than polished. Then the time came to audition. Both my parents worked, so my best friend came to the audition with me. All the other kids at the audition had their parents with them, praising them all the way to the doorway into the studio.

It saddened me that my parents weren't there but it set the tone for me believing that everything I had to do in life I would do on my own. The support was there but from afar. The tools I needed I had honed myself. I was ready.

I waited outside the audition studio at the SA Opera Theatre. I was nervous but I was practiced. I was a well-oiled machine. I knew I had this.

The door opened and my name was called. I stood up, sheet music in hand, and I walked into that audition space with confidence. I knew this song and I was well rehearsed. I stated my name to the panel of five people all staring at me. One man gave me a small smile, but the rest of the panel just stared at me, blankly. Goodness knows how many kids they were auditioning. How many stage parents waiting outside, how many wonderful and how many awful auditions they had to sit through.

No parents sitting outside for me; they'd left me to it. My bestie sat outside. I had this.

The panel asked me what song I had prepared, and I told them the song title. They seemed to prick their ears up when I mentioned the song. Not an aria for me, oh no, I wanted to give them something fun, boisterous and entertaining, because that reflected my personality. I looked over to the accompanist, nodded that I was ready, and I posed in the position I had practiced many times before. The piano started the opening bar, I opened my mouth and started to sing...

Preparation is key

> *When I first started out in the corporate sector, I doubted my experience.*

When I first started out in the corporate sector, I doubted my experience. When I looked at a job advert, if I didn't have 100% of the skills they required, I wouldn't apply. As I got older, I realised that this is not important. What is important is recognising the value that your unique perspective brings to a role.

Having a plan or at least the basic idea of a plan, the time is right to look at your transferable skills in greater depth. Too many times, people forget all of the great stuff they have achieved outside of the work place. Skills learnt doing a past time or hobby can lead to career paths you didn't think possible.

My basic plan:

1. Speak with as many people in my friendship circle as I can, who are currently working in the corporate space. Truly gain an understanding of what this work entails as I start to move into this sector. With more information comes informed decision making.

2. Be critical of my skills and write them down. Think of examples in my background to support my skills. Have these ready to add to my resume where needed.

3. Write a resume and get friends to review for relevance.

4. Research possible roles and companies that I want to apply for.

5. Apply for roles.

6. Take notes of what works to get an interview and what does not. Then make changes accordingly.

7. Revisit step 3 and update.

People are multifaceted and everything we learn makes us the people we will become. Don't pass by these opportunities. Think of how they may help you succeed in your overall goals. As I continue to forge my career, I have found that those skills learnt in my past have helped me become a better leader.

I think back to when I started singing in a choir, all I wanted to do was sing in the lead. I wanted my voice to be heard over everyone else. What I rapidly learnt was that in an ensemble, we all shine when we work together. When one person is trying to outshine everyone else, there is disharmony and this affects the entire group. Learning your place in the ensemble lets you shine in a different way and eventually you will be seen for what you bring to the team. The same can be said for your career and your workplace.

How you enter the room, how you curate your experience for an interview, every answer you give, every example you provide, every note you sing – it all matters.

When I was looking to move out of singing, and into a new career, I knew I would have to interview for a role. At some point I would have to tell someone about myself and how my singing skills would translate into my next role.

When I made the decision to pivot from singing to the corporate sector, I really had no idea what this would look like. I had to think very carefully about the skills I had and how they could be used.

Just as an audition, you generally only have one chance to impress. And believe me, first impressions count. How you enter the room, how you curate your experience for an interview, every answer you give, every example you provide, every note you sing – it all matters.

Part of my preparation was noting down all of my jobs including singing and the work required to support a singing career. Now this may sound strange but there is a lot of influencing, negotiation, planning and implementation needed to be a performer. For me it was about taking that knowledge and reframing it to meet the roles I applied for.

Reframe and reflect

Part of thinking differently was being able to reframe what I wanted. I had decisions to make to ensure that the path I was choosing would meet my needs. I needed to think about the type of career I was aspiring for. What was it I was seeking? I decided I needed to break this decision-making down into small achievable targets. In the very first instance I started to think about the industries that interested me, my preferred location, and my non-negotiables. This decision-making was hard; having only worked in performing and hospitality roles gave me no frame of reference for the corporate world. I tried to approach this decision-making through a lens of curiosity and joy, and to try to enjoy the process along the way.

Once I landed my first temping opportunity in the corporate world, I realised that there were a lot of things I didn't know and learning quickly was going to become

> *If I didn't know it, I would research it.*

standard. If I didn't know it, I would research it. I would ask all the questions I could and I would write copious amounts of notes. The learning phase gave me exceptional joy. It tapped into my curiosity and meant I had to learn new things, almost on a daily basis.

It was at this time that I developed a career reflection matrix based on my previous work experience and I used this to measure the amount of joy I was experiencing with every role I would continue to undertake. For the roles that weren't so joyful (and there were a few!), I didn't continue with them and for those that did, I stayed - but both types gave me the opportunity to and learn and grow.

To this day I still use this matrix, to ensure that the role I am in is still ticking all the right boxes. This matrix looks at the macro view of the role and does not focus on the days when things don't go to plan and you feel stressed or unhappy.

This matrix helps you determine whether the role overall is joyous and if you are challenged and still learning. It also helps to determine when it is time to leave a role, when you have learnt everything you needed to learn, and understand it's time to move on.

The career reflection matrix

The career reflection matrix is used in conjunction with the Role & Goal analysis. The order in which you use these is not fixed. They will help each other and therefore should be completed together. For me, it has always been important to focus on the joy a role has brought me and I am constantly revisiting this matrix.

The purpose of the career reflection matrix is to look at the following areas from a career perspective:

- Where you have come from

- What brought you joy in the roles you have held in the past

- What you enjoyed and what you did not enjoy

- What skills you have learnt along the way

- What skills are transferable to any new role

- Understanding what is valuable to you when undertaking a role.

- Where that next role might be, whether that is a step up, a lateral move or a shift to a different industry.

When Now, Means NOW!

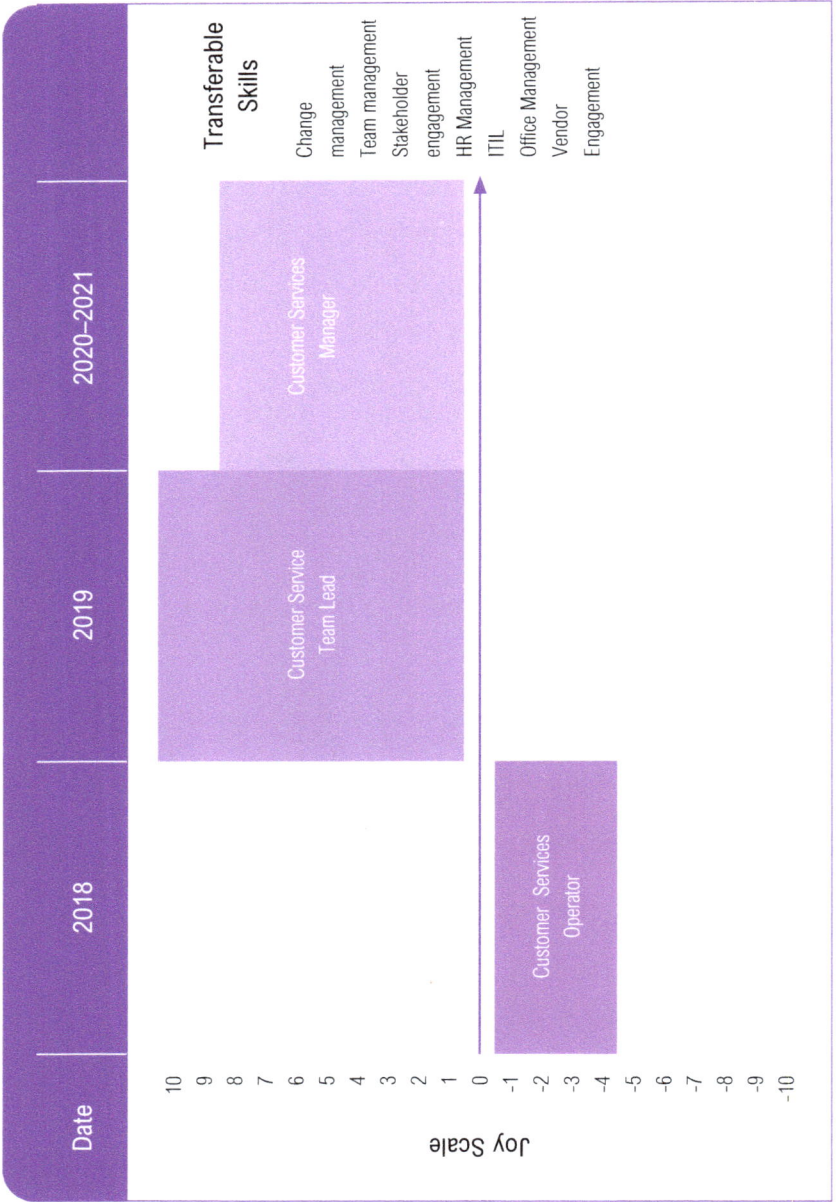

Date

	2018	2019	2020–2021	Transferable Skills

Joy Scale: 10, 9, 8, 7, 6, 5, 4, 3, 2, 1, 0, -1, -2, -3, -4, -5, -6, -7, -8, -9, -10

Customer Services Operator

Customer Service Team Lead

Customer Services Manager

Transferable Skills:
- Change management
- Team management
- Stakeholder engagement
- HR Management
- ITIL
- Office Management
- Vendor Engagement

Job Title	Customer Service Operator	Customer Service Lead	Customer Service Manager
Skills Learnt	Working with customer service support colleagues. Understanding the needs of the customer	Managing a small team of customer service agents Service KPIs Dealing with dissatisfied customers	Managing a large team of customer service agents Service KPIs Developing training programs to support my team
Reason for Joy Ranking	Highly stressed as the organization was going through a major change and no one knew what was happening. Customers were not getting the service they wanted and it required fielding excessive complaints.	Great organization Supportive and provided lots of training Fantastic inclusive team	Still the same great organization Supportive and provided lots of training Fantastic inclusive team
Game Changer	During this time I felt abandoned by the business and the leadership and I was determined to find another role that would help me grow and learn. I began to grow my network and reach out to other businesses that I was interested in working with.	I felt I had mastered team lead and my mentor arranged for me to meet with the divisional manager and I was offered a Customer Service Manager role.	Built a strong relationship with the GM of a different business unit so when an opportunity for a different role became available I was able to apply and win that role.
Training	Customer Service CRM training ITIL	Team management People management	HR Management Office management

Date

| 2018 | 2019 | 2020–2021 |

Transferable Skills

Change management
Team management
Stakeholder engagement
HR Management
ITIL
Office Management
Vendor Engagement

Customer Services Manager

Customer Service Team Lead

Customer Services Operator

Joy Scale

10
9
8
7
6
5
4
3
2
1
0
-1
-2
-3
-4
-5
-6
-7
-8
-9
-10

Step 1 Understanding the Scale

The joy scale represents every role you have ever held, the year in which you held it and how much joy this brought to you or how much joy it took away. This is purely a subjective scale of how the role made you feel whether that made you feel extremely satisfied or extremely dissatisfied.

If you are new to the work force, this matrix can still be used. Think about the things you do in your daily life. The things you learnt from school, the things you learnt from growing up, from your friends, parents, coaches and the like. There is joy all around you and this matrix is designed to help you think about joy in the things that you do.

Start completing the template. To make this a little easier work backwards from your latest role. Before starting on the template make a note of the roles you have held and the rough time period in each – I use years, however it could be a monthly measurement if you contract or are just starting out in your career.

As you think about the roles think about joy they brought or didn't bring and think about why you are ranking them in that way.

As you think about the roles think about joy they brought or didn't bring and think about why you are ranking them in that way. Really think about the roles and be critical of them. How a role and an organisation left you feeling is very important.

There will always be elements of a role or organisation that was frustrating or challenging. Moments when your time may not have been joyous, but on the whole, for the entire time you worked there, how would you measure it.

Personally, I try to not think of past roles with rose colored glasses.

Personally, I try to not think of past roles with rose colored glasses. I revisit my journals to remember how I was feeling at the time and this does help me to be truly critical of each role. This gives me the best insight to my past roles which helps me consider my directions for future roles.

Step 2 Enter job titles

The first step in any journey - enter the job role titles in to the template.

Job Title	e.g. Customer Service operator	e.g. Customer Service Team Lead

Step 3 Skills learnt

We start to get into the meaty bit of the template. You begin by brain storming all of the skills you learnt in each role. You may find it easier to work from most recent and then go back. You can jump around in the template as things come to mind. There is no need to be linear here. Just try to capture as much as you can.

Skills Learnt	e.g. Working with customer service support colleagues. Understanding the needs of the customer	e.g. Managing a small team of customer service agents. Service KPIs. Dealing with dissatisfied customers

Step 4 Enter the reason you have ranked the role as you have in the joy section

I want you to think back to why you gave the particular roles the ranking that you gave them. How did they bring joy? Are there any common themes here that you can take away from this.

Reason for Joy Ranking	e.g. Highly stressed as the organisation was going through a major change and no one knew what was happening. Customers were not getting the service they wanted and it required fielding excessive complaints.	e.g. Great organisation Supportive and provided lots of training. Fantastic inclusive team.

Step 5 Understanding what the game changer was in the role

The game change is an interesting section and for me requires the most thought. In this section I want you to think about what took place in this role that enabled you to expedite your career. What was the game changer enabling you to jump to a more challenging role or to get a promotion or to really understand what your non-negotiables were.

I believe that just knowing what you are not prepared to do enables you to focus on anything else.

Game Changer	e.g., During this time, I felt abandoned by the business and the leadership and I was determined to find another role that would help me grow and learn. I began to grow my network and reach out to other businesses that I was interested in working with.	e.g., I felt I had mastered team lead and my mentor arranged for me to meet with the divisional manager and I was offered a Customer Service Manager role.

Step 6 Acknowledging the training and certifications awarded in a role

The training and qualification section should be an easy one to complete. Note down any formal or informal training you may have done. Items with a qualification as well as items that were run internally in your organization that added to your skill set.

Training	e.g., Customer Service CRM training ITIL	e.g., Team Management People Management CRM Configuration

Step 7 Noting transferable skills

Now finally, look at the roles you have worked in and look at the transferable skills that you have and list all of these. Every item you write here adds to your tool box and means that you are more than just your current or previous role.

Transferable Skills	e.g., Change Management
	Team Management
	Stakeholder Management
	HR Management
	ITIL
	Office Management
	Vendor Engagement

The key goal behind the career reflection matrix is in helping you see what you have achieved. It is a way to celebrate where you have come from and then open your thinking to new opportunities. The completion of this matrix will help you in your transition plan. It will also provide you with collateral to add to your resume.

Combine this with the outcomes of the Role and Goal analysis and you are well on your way to making that career transition you have been seeking.

Making the move

Making that elusive career transition may feel daunting at first but it reminds me of the times I would audition for shows. When you are looking to make a change, you need to do your research, you need to rehearse. You need to understand the

When you are looking to make a change, you need to do your research, you need to rehearse.

organisation and role you will be interviewing for.

For auditions, I would look at the style of music and this would then determine the songs I would rehearse. The songs to choose were the ones that would show my greatest range. Similarly, to the skills and transferable skills you will demonstrate at an interview. Choosing the best song to highlight your voice is the same as ensuring that you have the best examples for your interview.

When interviewing you will want think of the best examples of your experience whilst also focusing on your transferable skills. We all have transferable skills and

> *When interviewing you will want think of the best examples of your experience whilst also focusing on your transferable skills.*

understanding how they will help to differentiate you from other candidates is vital in standing out.

From my background as a performer, I initially needed to link my transferable skills in a way that would help me to be taken seriously. Remember that I was coming from a performance background and I needed to be able to bring all aspects of the music industry into view.

There were many times that the interviewer only wanted to know about singing and they were not really interested in my transferable skills. I was a novelty and I needed to be able to get past this. That was the first hurdle and one I believe many people experience throughout their careers.

As I have progressed in male dominated industries, I face very similar draw backs when interviewing for roles. I am less a novelty more a minority and I have been faced with similar biases along the way. The key for me has been to always look for the best way to improve for the next interview. Coming from a performance background, there are many more people wanting the coveted role on stage than there are roles to fill. You learn to deal with disappointment and learning ways to improve for the next time.

Here is an example of how I linked transferable skills from my performance background when interviewing for my first corporate roles:

- **Working under pressure** - performing in front of live audiences enabled me to work under pressure. If something went wrong on stage, I just needed to deal with it and know that the performance must go on. Having examples of how to handle this needed to be readily available.

- **Planning** a performance schedule meant that I had to ensure the best paying gigs were given priority, but also knowing that some lesser-paying gigs could potentially lead to a regular weekly time slot. This meant less work having to schedule and audition for new gigs. Being able to see the big picture was important.

- **Logistics** are vital when performing. You need to know where you are going and when you need to be there. You need to have your stage gear collected and packed and you absolutely cannot be late for the show. Set up time and sound checks need to be considered.

- **Executing** the performance to meet the needs of the audience is as important as landing the gig. If you are singing at a wedding, you had better be certain to have enough slow songs to dance to at the beginning of the set and enough dance numbers at the end for when the crowd want it. Many performers work on referrals and having happy clients means more work. Execution is absolutely imperative to getting more work.

To make the transition, I decided my best option was to do temporary assignments. This way I would have access to various organisations and could start building a picture of what I liked and what I did not. The key was to get a temping agency to take a chance on me with my limited business experience but a tonne of transferable skills.

Temping assignments enabled me to connect with many different people, enjoy learning new skills and helped me decide exactly what type of work I would eventually end up doing. In the corporate world today, this is the same for contract work. You can work for a short period of time and decide if that organisation or similar are what you are seeking. You can learn new skills and make connections and you can move on to the next role until you decide what you want.

And to put you out of your misery, I landed that role in the SA Youth Opera. I met some wonderful people; some I am still in contact with to this day. All of us have moved on in various

You can work for a short period of time and decide if that organisation or similar are what you are seeking.

ways, some stayed in performing and others transitioned into corporate life. Back then we all wanted the same thing and now we still do. We want to know we are making a difference, enjoying our career choices and experiencing joy, every day.

Key Takeaways:

- *Every skill will link in some way to you career path, you just need to think of how.*

- *Research is the foundation for everything you will undertake.*

- *Every connection will add to your network.*

- *Know that we are not all that different from one another, we all want the same things in the end.*

The Importance of Networking and Sponsorship

As a member of the C-Suite, I cannot tell you how important networking and sponsorship is. Recently having connected with a fellow CIO who had decided to leave the corporate world and branch out on his own, the one thing he said was how much he regretted not nurturing his network and building greater sponsorship whilst in a role. As he declined multiple invitations to build his network, he was slowly limiting his potential reach. Starting his own consultancy business meant he would have to start rebuilding his network.

You never know the power of your network until you really need it.

Starting your networking journey

When I landed my first temping job, this was on the back of networking. I didn't realise it at the time, but meeting someone who had seen me perform enabled me to weave my transferable skills into the conversation. Just as with an interview, having something prepared that you can draw upon is vital. When networking it will be your elevator pitch. In less than 30 seconds tell them something about yourself that makes them want to hear more.

> *When networking it will be your elevator pitch. In less than 30 seconds tell them something about yourself that makes them want to hear more.*

Where that first impression in an interview was important, the networking was the ice breaker that gave me the opportunity to engage in a conversation that until then I was unable to effectively have. Instead of my background being seen as a hinderance it was seen in a completely different light because I had broken the ice (inadvertently) before-hand.

When I started working in the corporate world, I knew that I needed to think about each step carefully. I did not want my career to simply happen to me, I wanted to take control of it. There is nothing more dissatisfying than falling into the next unfulfilling role. Just like being on the gig treadmill, I did not want this for my burgeoning corporate career.

I needed to plan out my networking strategy and ensure that I was meeting with the right people who would be able to help build on my very young career. Working in a temping capacity meant that I was able to attend networking events sponsored by the temping agency. This was my first attempt at networking.

The first thing I noticed about the agency events is that they were focused on bringing all the temporary employees together. They were people in the same situation as I was in and we were able to discuss the types of assignments we were on and what we were hoping to achieve. What this did not give me was an opportunity for advancement.

I swiftly realised that if I wanted to move my career aspirations along, I needed some advice. I needed someone who would help me navigate the networking circuit and help me meet the right people to help me.

Know the power of sponsorship

Having connected so well with Cheryl, the woman who interviewed me for the temping work, I decided to reach out to her and ask her advice. By this stage I had been temping for over 6 months and had built a strong reputation as someone the company could count on. When I reached out to her, I explained my dilemma. I wanted more and I wanted to network with people that would be able to help me.

To my surprise she was more than happy to help me not just with networking advice, but more targeted advice that I use to this day.

She advised me to do the following things:

- **Know your purpose** – Be passionate when you speak about it. If you could summarise your experience into 3 sentences, what would you say?

- **Choose the right event** – don't attend every event out there. Be discerning. By looking at the event and the type of people that would be attending allows you to focus on the level of individual. Focusing on the decision makers means that you can reach out to them in the future, and they can reach out to you.

- **Cultivate a sponsor** – It's important to have someone who will advocate for you, someone who can put you forward for new opportunities. It was at this moment that I realised that Cheryl was my very first sponsor. Whenever there was a problem client, I was the first person she would reach out to, I would placate the customer and smooth things over, especially when another temp did not perform to expectations. Eventually I would get my very first fulltime role through Cheryl's sponsorship.

What I eventually grew to realise is that a good sponsor is like a good artists agent. You both have some skin in the game. The sponsor is putting their reputation on the line for you and in turn you are putting your own reputation on the line.

As I have grown in my career, my sponsors have changed and grown with me. They represent different career pathways and different organisations. What they all have in common is an intrinsic knowledge of the value I bring to an organisation. They only know this because I have talked about it and I have demonstrated this throughout my career.

A sponsor does not have to stay with you throughout your career, but if you are lucky enough, they will eventually become your friend and this is where the magic of relationships happens.

Build your support squad

In a corporate environment you will also build a support squad. These will be the people who will have your back, who will listen and provide support. They can be your sponsors, your mentors, your coaches, your peers, your team and anyone in-between. The important thing is to recognise them and to foster your relationship with them.

Your relationship with your squad will be two-way. There will be times when they support you and times when you will support them.

Your relationship with your squad will be two-way. There will be times when they support you and times when you will support them. This, like every other relationship, needs to grow and be nurtured and just when you think it is solid enough, it will need to be nurtured some more. In order to do this, you need to ensure that you have a strategy in place to ensure that you are growing and nurturing this aspect of your network.

The main way I have found to build and grow a healthy squad is to be generous with my time. Being generous with your time is often more valuable to your squad than money. The things they will learn from you and you will learn from them will ensure continuing success for both of you.

> *The main way I have found to build and grow a healthy squad is to be generous with my time. Being generous with your time is often more valuable to your squad than money.*

When I was at a cross roads in my career, I wasn't sure which way I wanted to go. I was heavily invested in Transport and Logistics but wasn't happy with an operational role. I had a member of my squad who thought that my personality, attention to detail and business acumen would suit a business analyst role. From squad member to sponsor was a small step but meant so much to me.

At the time I had no idea what a business analyst did let alone know how to do this work. Again, those transferable skills came in to action. Having a sponsor enabled a change into a new career opportunity within Information

Technology. Had I known then what I do now, I would have hugged him even harder when the opportunity arose. A coffee and regular catch ups will have to suffice.

My sponsor put me in front of a business associate and sold my skills to this new potential employer. What I had was my passion, my love of learning and I had learnt to actively listen. I listened to the business problem trying to be solved and I contributed to the discussion with how my skills would enable me to address the problem. Had this introduction and subsequent role not have taken place, I may not be in the C-Suite now.

Knowing and having the skills alone is not enough. The people you meet and engage with may be the contact you need for a future event that you do not see coming. Every contact and every sponsor may help propel your career further in ways you may not have ever imagined. I certainly never imagined the C-Suite on that faithful day I landed my first temp job yet here I am.

Construct your network

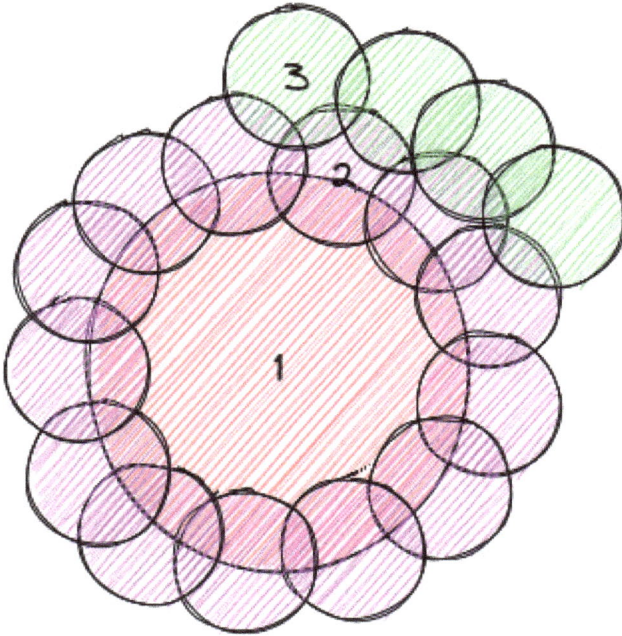

Constructing your network in summary:

1. Start small, each layer will link to the next layer and the next layer and so on

2. Invest time in growing your network

3. Write down your networking objectives:

    a. Plan out who you want to meet and think about why

    b. How many people per month would you like to connect with

    c. What areas of expertise do they have that is of interest

    d. What areas of expertise do you have that they may find interesting

4. Don't rush. Building a network is about building a real connection. This is not about the number of followers you have.

5. Nurture your network. Think of it as a garden that needs to be watered regularly to flourish.

6. Embrace the discomfort of networking. It is never easy at the start but it will grow on you.

7. Never be afraid to share your network with others, that is ultimately what networking is.

Your network will become the most powerful thing you will have in the corporate world but understanding what makes up your network will help you when planning out your networking approach.

Know the difference

Having a support squad is imperative to making your network work for you. However, there are differences between each layer in your network and sometimes they are not mutually exclusive.

> *Having a support squad is imperative to making your network work for you.*

Here are the definitions that you should become familiar with and some ideas on how to engage each level.

Sponsor

A sponsor will present themselves to you, so be on the lookout. When a sponsor is interested in what you have to say and asks probing questions about your career path, take this as a sign. I have never asked someone to be a sponsor for me. It just seems to have happened. I get asked a lot about how to get a sponsor; all I can say to this is actively listen.

When you meet someone and are truly interested in what they say and they are interested in what you are saying then this can lead to sponsorship. Continue to cultivate the relationship but not with an agenda of landing a new role or being sponsored but purely out of curiosity and wanting human connection.

- A sponsor is that individual or individuals who have the ability to progress your career aspirations. They are generally well connected and have their own extensive network.

- A sponsor will see something in you that perhaps you do not see and they can see how you may add value to someone else in their network.

- A sponsor will discuss your attributes within their network and may facilitate an introduction.

How sponsorship helped me:

This took place when I was working for a distribution company. My contract was coming to an end and I was starting to feel very unsure of my next step. This particular sponsor was discussing my skillset with an associate who was looking for someone to support his company as a business analyst. I wasn't exactly doing that work but my sponsor felt that my transferable skills would slot right in.

My sponsor arranged an introduction over a coffee and I was able to explain my background, what I was hoping to achieve and the value I thought I could bring to the business. I was successful and commenced at the end of my contract. If it wasn't for this opportunity, I do not think I would be in the CIO seat now. This was the start of a journey I had no idea I was about to embark upon.

The thing I remember the most from the early days in my career was remaining curious and parking fear to the side. Every closed door on one side opened a more interesting door on the other. I remained positive and became more and more aware of the value I could bring.

Mentor

If I were to use an analogy from my current working environment, I would say that a coach helps you win the game but a mentor helps you win the season.

- A mentor is the one person that you can speak to about your career aspirations. They are focused on your career, not on the day to day of your job.

- A mentor will challenge your thinking, help you explore the sort of career you want to have and will help you see how you may navigate the transitions within your career.

- Mentors will come and go as your career progresses. The intention of a good mentor is to know when it is time for you to move on from them.

How mentorship helped me:

I have had the privilege of having multiple mentors in my career. Sometimes I will have a couple of mentors at the same time. This is because I have different mentors for different avenues of my career. One mentor to assist me with my career aspirations within my current work place and then the mentors that are outside of the workplace that are helping me achieve different goals.

I had a mentor when I was first working for a major transportation company in Australia. He enabled me to improve my leadership style by seeing that I would be a good leader if given the chance. He guided me through the interview process for a new leadership role which was outside of my area of expertise.

He reminded me once again of my transferable skills and was with me every step of the way as I transitioned from a Senior Business Analyst role into a Service Level Manager role. He questioned my decision making and helped me to build an amazing team to support the work I was doing. He explained the importance of a strong team and helped me learn how to recruit the best talent.

To this day I am grateful to all of the advice he gave me as without his support and kind but stern words I do not think I would be as good a leader as I am today.

Coach

As mentioned, I believe that a coach will help you win the game. By this I mean that they will be there to help you unpick the problems on a day-to-day basis. Your coach is your line manager or the equivalent of this in your organisation.

- A coach will help you with solving problems that arise within your team or with a colleague.

- They will see things from a different perspective and help you to make the best decision you can with the available information you have at the time.

- A coach will be aware of the intimate functions of the business you work within and will be able to add context to the advice they give you to assist you in making the best decisions you can.

How coaching helped me:

I have had many line managers throughout my career. Some better than others but all with a unique perspective on problems that I needed to solve. In hindsight, when I have had line managers whom I felt were not up to snuff, I felt very distressed by this and it would fester into animosity for me.

What I have grown to recognise is that we are all on our own leadership journey and if a line manager doesn't resonate with you, there are still things you can learn from the experience. Keep your mind open to the possibilities and if you really do not connect with your line manager you can make the decision to move on.

My favourite coaching moment was when I was leading a highly technical team and I knew that the team members did not respect me. I do not come from a highly technical background, but I have spent the last 20+ years honing my leadership skills and this I am very proud of.

My coach at the time said to me that the best thing for me to do was to not worry about the technical but remain steadfast in my approach to help develop my new leaders. They would learn so much more from me on how to be the best leaders they could be and that this would ultimately be my legacy.

My coach said that technology changes so rapidly but the way people respond and lead does not. Teach the team to lead and they will continue to have fruitful careers. It's funny that as I have progressed in my career, I face this challenge in all roles. When I get to the end of a role and am about to move on from a business, I receive the same feedback from my team, especially from those that originally did not rate me.

That feedback warms my heart - "You have been the best leader I have ever had"

To this day as I look at my ever-growing network, I see those ex-team members and have them still reach out to me today. That is the legacy my coach told me about and I am so grateful that I can pay it forward.

Colleague

Finally, you will have colleagues that may become coaches, mentors and even sponsors as they grow in their careers. The key thing for me is to make meaningful connections with my colleagues, in fact I like to make meaningful connections across my network. It is not a numbers game for me. I want to take meaning out of every interaction and make them worthwhile for both of us.

- A colleague is the person in your organisation who you will connect with and be able to share war stories with.

- A colleague may eventually become your friend for many years to come.

- A colleague may become a member of your support squad.

How collegiate connection has helped me:

I remember my father saying to me that as you get older it is harder to make friends. I always thought about this comment as strange. When I was younger and performing, I had a lot of friends and I still have quite a few of them to this day.

I believe that cultivating friendships is similar to cultivating a garden. You have to water it to nurture it, you have to remain actively involved in it and you have to put in the effort. It is not hard to make friends as you get older but it does take effort.

The same can be said for building relationships with colleagues. I do this regularly and I love the interactions. I make a point to catch up with people from my previous roles, whether that be virtually, over coffee or for a meal. It takes time but I love hearing how their careers have changed, what they are doing now and what they hope to achieve further along their journey.

The personal connection that I have with colleagues is what makes my career so successful. I am grateful for the opportunity to have every interaction that I do and I make the time. This is the most important factor: make the time.

Having wonderful connections with people has made my career a supreme joy and when you measure joy the way I do, then this is a very important factor. This element takes pride of place in my career reflection matrix. As I

Having wonderful connections with people has made my career a supreme joy and when you measure joy the way I do, then this is a very important factor.

have progressed in my career, I have grown my network. Is my network as large as some? no it isn't, but it has been cultivated and grown with care, it has been watered regularly and it has enabled me to enjoy my career to date and make some wonderful friendships along the way.

Key Takeaways:

- *Know your purpose, you will always need this.*

- *Be as generous with your time as your sponsors will be with theirs.*

- *Actively listen when networking.*

- *Well-maintained connections will last a lifetime.*

- *Don't be afraid to lose a sponsor, some are with you for a long time and some are not.*

- *Be open to friendships, your network doesn't always have to be about work.*

Practice Gives Power

When I was sixteen my father dedicated his time to setting up the first South Australian Gridiron Association (SAGA). My family immigrated from the United States when I was a baby and for the last sixteen years my father missed his favourite sport.

Whenever the Super Bowl was televised on Australian TV, he would be up watching it, no matter what the time. VCRs were commercially available by then, but they were too expensive, so my parents would stay up to watch the game regardless of how late it was. My father felt so passionately about the sport that he wanted to bring a little bit of home to Australia. He began working on the founding committee for SAGA and set up a team in the Southern region. They were originally called the Southern Longhorns, with colours of burnt orange and white. Later they would change their name to the Southern Oilers and when my father passed away, the entire team wore black armbands in memory of him.

When I was sixteen, however, I was working on my singing career. My skin condition was relatively under control, and no more extended hospital visits were necessary. I had been performing solidly at this stage, when the opportunity to perform at the opening game of the first season of the gridiron association presented itself. The committee was looking for someone to sing the Australian National Anthem at the commencement of the first game and my father suggested me.

No audition was necessary as my father said I would do it and the price matched the committee's budget. I was free, exactly the price that they wanted to pay. Afterall, it didn't really matter how terrible I was, as the committee had no idea whether anyone would come to watch a relatively unknown sport in Australia.

From my sixteen-year-old perspective, however, this would be one of the most defining moments of my life. I learnt more about first impressions in this moment than I would at any other time in my career.

Ruminating doesn't help

There is nothing more daunting than singing in front of a large crowd, but add to it singing the National Anthem and my nerves were much worse than normal. At sixteen I had a lot of bravado. Even if I couldn't do something, I would still throw my hat in the ring. It just meant that I would have to work a little harder to be ready. That strategy didn't work out quite so well for me when I said I could tap dance. Just to be clear, I could not and have never been able to tap dance, but at sixteen, I thought how hard could it be? Let's just say, very bloody hard.

> *At sixteen I had a lot of bravado. Even if I couldn't do something, I would still throw my hat in the ring.*

The evening my father came home from one of his committee meetings, he was more excited than usual. He called me into the kitchen to announce that I had won this gig. He was very pleased with himself and I was mortified. Now I had to prove myself to a huge audience and not embarrass my father. I was more frightened than I could have imagined but I wanted my father's approval so badly that all I could do was rejoice in his excitement. In reality I was really scared.

This was one of those moments when I realised that there was no wriggle room for error. When you sing live in front of a crowd you had better get it right because there are no second chances. This is how a wedding photographer must feel. You have one day to get things right and you can't mess it up.

This is the same with first impressions, once they are set it is very hard to change them. How often have you met someone, made a mess of the introduction and the relationship is ruined before it had a chance.

I knew that I had to get this right, in my sixteen-year-old brain I felt a lot riding on this. For one thing my father believed I could do it and that was enough for me. Wanting to make him proud of me was very important, he was a professional musician after all and this is what I wanted to be. If I couldn't get this right then my burgeoning musical career would certainly be over.

I found myself spending endless hours ruminating on every possible scenario. The good ones, the bad ones and the truly horrific ones. This did not help with preparations as I became fixated on failure. Then the self-doubt started to creep in. I didn't have a plan to deal with how I was feeling. I needed advice and I needed it quickly.

The best advice ever

I remember feeling alone and the pressure was building. I didn't know what to do about my anxiety and I asked my best friend for her advice. She said "Remember who you are, what you have already achieved and use it."

As my preparations began, I remembered my best friend's advice. I focused on the lyrics in the first instance. Getting these wrong would be a disaster (and who knew that the Australian National Anthem had two verses that needed to be performed - I certainly didn't at the time). This seemed more daunting to me than anything else, that and not quite understanding what "girt" meant (girt is from the Old English "gird" meaning to surround or encircle. In other words, Australia is surrounded by sea. Who knew!).

Once again, I intended to practice every day to ensure that I knew every nuance of this song. To be honest it is a little dry but the impending performance was very important. I had to do my parents proud and get it right and there was a part of me that felt obligated to do this well for my friends who couldn't.

> *My entire life has been punctuated by moments where I have felt like I have wanted to give up. The rejections from auditions were replaced by the rejections at interviews.*

My entire life has been punctuated by moments where I have felt like I have wanted to give up. The rejections from auditions were replaced by the rejections at interviews. My career not moving as fast as my ambitions and the feeling that time is running out, always in the back of my mind. However, I am always brought back to my closest childhood friends and the reality that they will never have the opportunities I am wanting to give up. It is at that moment that I stop, pause, reflect and get back on the treadmill.

Day after day of practice and reviewing the lyrics until I felt, once again, like a well-oiled machine. Then finally the Saturday of the inaugural game came around. To say I was nervous was an understatement. Even having performed for a number of years at this stage, I still got a little stage fright. Having built this up in my mind made it much worse, but I remembered that advice.

"Remember who you are"

As I sat in the locker rooms waiting for the teams to run out onto the playing field I felt as if I were having an out of body experience. I watched the clock in the change rooms, slowly tick as if everything was in slow motion. I felt sick to my stomach, my palms started sweating and my mouth went very dry. How could I sing when I could barely breathe?

I stood up in the locker room and practiced some scales. I took a sip of warm water and did some more scales. I whispered the lyrics to myself and I paced the floor until the time came to walk out onto the field. If I think back hard enough, I can still feel the fear creep up inside me as I walked out from the locker rooms.

If I was going to do this professionally, I had to get this right, every performance had to be right. No wriggle room for failure, no space for the wrong note or wrong lyric, it had to be perfect. No pressure!

No wriggle room for failure, no space for the wrong note or wrong lyric, it had to be perfect. No pressure!

Perfection is a myth

I walked out to my introduction by the president of the South Australian Grid Iron Association, "And here to sing the National Anthem..." The crowd politely applauded as I walked up to the microphone. The turnout was much larger than I had anticipated. The stands were full and the audience stood in anticipation of the National Anthem.

Once again, as I had done so many times before, I planted my feet and I held my head high. I looked up into the bleachers and saw the expectant faces and I started to sing...

"Australians all let us rejoice for we are young and free..."

I sang my heart out, both verses, pitch perfect, in key, timed perfectly, no embellishment. Just sang the song as it was originally intended to be performed, but I had made a minor mistake in the second verse. When I had finished, the crowd applauded and I walked off of the field. No one seemed to notice the mistake, but I knew.

More than 30 hours of practice for less than a 3-minute performance and I made a mistake. As I made my way back to the locker area, I had the president of the association walk up to me and my first thought was, oh no, he knows about the mistake! However, he just congratulated me for a wonderful performance.

I wasn't sure how to take this compliment, after all there was that mistake, but I said thank you and made my way back to the locker room. When the first half of the game was over, so many people filtered back in to the locker rooms and this is when it happened.

Every player, cheer leader and support staff came up to me and told me how well I had performed. They were astonished that this sound had come out of my mouth. None of them knew I was a singer and they thought my performance was wonderful. Many said they would remember this for years to come.

For me I was fixated on the mistake and couldn't really enjoy the accolades. I kept going over the verse in my mind. I knew the lyrics; I was well-oiled so how did I miss this?

This was when I realised that although first impressions count, most people will not recognise little mix ups. The perfectionist within us is of our own making and not from other people. The pressure we place on ourselves is forged out of our internal desires to be the very best. To this day,

The perfectionist within us is of our own making and not from other people. The pressure we place on ourselves is forged out of our internal desires to be the very best.

when something doesn't go to plan, I get that niggling little feeling in my gut and I just have to push it aside. No one is perfect, you may have perfect moments, perfect days, but there is no consistency in perfection, instead there is power in practice.

📝 Key Takeaways:

- *Practice gives power, be well honed but embrace your imperfection.*

- *Remember your journey, it has shaped you and will continue to shape you.*

- *Ruminating wastes the time you could be learning.*

- *Remember you are not alone, we all feel moments of stage fright, just breathe, plant your feet and take it away.*

Having the Team to Back You Up

My first leadership gig

After several years of working in the office temp space, I finally landed my first leadership role. I was not expecting this and I had no idea what a manager, let alone a leader, needed to do. I had been the lead singer in bands but this felt very different to me.

The key differences were apparent as soon as my role was announced to the business. In a band, you are looking for individuals who are into similar music as yourself. Each of you has a different role to play in the band. If you're the drummer or the bassist, you are the rhythm section and you keep time for everyone else. If you are the lead guitarist you set the melody. If you're the lead singer, you express the lyrics. Each of you knows what your place is within the band. Having auditioned, you have displayed

> *No one knew anything about me, I couldn't sing to prove my worth, I had to lead to prove it.*

your capability to do the job and you have been chosen above others.

In an office it is similar but there are many differences which made my first leadership role very challenging. I was in my early twenties and I was managing a group of people who were thirty years my seniors. They saw me as a child, and they weren't wrong, but they also lacked respect for the role I was given. I had no credibility with this team. I was interviewed for the role but not one of my team were part of that interview process.

When I was singing, I commanded respect because I could lead the band. I had talent and this is what I brought to the band. In the corporate world, I was the office temp who was promoted to a leadership role. No one knew anything about me, I couldn't sing to prove my worth, I had to lead to prove it.

In this first leadership role, I was leading a group of courier drivers, fifty plus in age, all men. To say I was a little intimidated is an understatement. I honestly had no idea what to do to lead these men. I was young and ambitious but that doesn't mean I wasn't scared.

My first day was hard but it wasn't the hardest. Everything was alien to me and being able to sing wasn't getting me through this. What I needed was to understand the people working for me. What I did know was that the best way to learn was to listen. In a band, you need to listen to the music, feel the rhythm, know when to come in and when to stop. This is really the same when learning about people.

Listen and learn, and when you think you know it all, listen some more. Know that it is not about you, it is about them. What I learnt in those first few weeks really surprised me. The men that were reporting in to me were just as scared of me as I was of them. I was an unknown quantity and they were afraid that I would make changes that would impact their livelihoods. I was young and had no transport experience and this intimidated them even more.

The rationale as to why I was leading them didn't make sense and they needed to understand this. My first action as a leader was to explain why I was appointed.

Defining the strategy

The reason for my appointment was simple. I had a keen interest in technology and proved this whilst working as a temp. If there was a computer problem, I would step in and solve it. I wasn't afraid of technology and in a time when technology was very new and very scary, that gave me an advantage. The role was supporting the technology work the transport company I worked for had been contracted to do.

I was not managing a fleet of standard courier drivers. I was leading a team of drivers who were employed to exchange EFTPOS (electronic funds transfer) devices. When I first started working in the corporate world, EFT was a brand-new service. It was not something that every shop keeper had. The devices were large and clunky, the technology new and unreliable. If you think back to mobile phones when they first entered the market place, you will understand what I mean.

The role of my department was the tracking and exchange of these devices across the Australian state that I was working in. Strict service levels needed to be adhered to as this was part of the financial sector and the drivers were the ones who would undertake the exchanges.

My first few days were spent trying to have conversations with a team that were not happy with my appointment. They were not interested in helping me learn, or helping me to understand what they did. I was like a mosquito, buzzing around their heads, making a lot of noise and not helping in any way. Every day was more miserable than the next.

I began to doubt my competency and felt like giving up, when something extraordinary happened to change this.

I began to doubt my competency and felt like giving up, when something extraordinary happened to change this.

I was contacted by one of our customers who was very dissatisfied with the service they were receiving and were contemplating moving to another provider. This announcement to the team was frightening, as this particular customer was a major one. With this loss the department would most definitely be downsized, impacting quite a few employees.

There was panic, and suddenly each of the team began to come to me, willing to help me learn. I needed to understand exactly what we did, what our service agreements were and what we were missing that caused such dissatisfaction with our customer. What I did know was if one customer was unhappy then more would follow.

I needed to have a strategy for my team, it needed to have a vision of service excellence and everyone needed to understand it and be on board with it. We needed to be performing from the same set list.

I put a strategy together, and I worked with the team on this. I knew from being in a band that we all needed to have some say but eventually the final say would be with me. Some concessions would be made but overall, the outcome had to be to retain our customers.

This was my first output as a leader. A strategic plan that would ensure we retained our customers, exceeded their expectations and grew the department to ensure roles were maintained.

Once I had the strategic plan, I then went to meet with all of my customers. I took them through my strategic plan, how I would report against it and the company's commitment to them. The meetings went well, generally. Some of the customers were still unhappy, as the service had been quite poor for some time, but they were willing to give me time to implement my strategy.

All of this took place in my first month, in my first leadership role. The one thing I did realise, without having any leadership training, was the importance of vision. The team needed to understand their role within the company and how important it was to maintain relationships with the customers we worked for.

Taking everyone on the journey

Whether you are leading a band or leading a business, you will always have to take people on the strategic journey. You have to explain your why and you will need to do so in a way that everyone feels consulted. It shouldn't have to take a near catastrophe to get buy in, but sometimes this can help.

In my first foray into leadership, I learnt the importance of "what's in it for me". This is the one thing that a leader needs to be able to tap into for each person in their team. This can only be learned by actively listening and having in-depth conversations.

When I was first leading, I made the mistake of assuming that the reason my team disliked my appointment was because I was young. Age had nothing to do with it. The men in my team were simply afraid of the changes that were to come with a new leader. It would not have mattered what my age was. I represented the unknown and they were scared.

When the customer complaint came in, I had an opportunity to take them on the journey with me and in doing so, I managed to get their buy in. They felt part of the development of the strategy and they believed that they would be able to achieve it.

I learned that assumptions are dangerous and giving people the benefit of the doubt in the first place can help you in the long run.

In every role, since that first role, I have done the same thing. I spend the first month actively listening to my team members. I understand their goals and aspirations, what they want to achieve in the organisation, what works and what does not. I listen and note this and then I start to flesh out the strategy for the team, taking into consideration my observations from those initial meetings.

I learned that assumptions are dangerous and giving people the benefit of the doubt in the first place can help you in the long run.

Key Takeaways:

- *You don't need to like the same things, however appreciating each other's differences strengthens rapport.*

- *The journey is best enjoyed with others.*

- *Assumptions come from fear, learn before assuming.*

- *Others may see your potential, so go with it.*

Taking Direction

In my corporate career, I have had many bosses. Just like everyone else, some have been wonderful and others not so much. I personally believe that if I can learn from my boss and they feel they can learn from me then it will be a productive relationship.

When I was younger and performing, it was very hard for me to take feedback. I always felt that this was criticising my craft. I felt that I had worked so hard that I could not possibly improve. How wrong I was. What I did not realise at the time was that feedback is meant to help you improve, even if the improvement is the smallest thing, every little bit helps.

When I had moved to Melbourne, I had the opportunity to work as a backing singer in a small recording studio. I had recorded in studios in my past, when singing with large ensembles but to have a gig where I was hired to sing backing vocals for bands that would pay me was something new.

I remember meeting the audio engineer for the first time and being shown to the sound booth. It was foreign to me and I felt ill at ease. I knew I could sing; I could belt out a song and be heard at the back of an auditorium but this style of singing was very different.

My first run through was terrible. I had not had much experience and I thought I needed to impress and that louder was better. In a recording studio it isn't necessarily the case.

The engineer was great and he came into the sound booth and gave me some feedback that I will not forget. He said, just relax into the music, let your voice flow naturally and don't try to impress, just sing for you.

His manner was so caring and non-judgemental that I took this feedback and I did exactly what he suggested. I just sang for me.

I then became a permanent fixture at the recording studio and from there joined my first Melbourne band.

In a management role you are constantly providing observations and needing team members to take this on board. I learnt very early on how important the messaging is and how important it is to take direction yourself. When faced with missing an objective or failing to meet a goal, direction is likely to help you salvage your plan and achieve your outcomes. As a leader it is the difference between someone leaving the business because of your lack of leadership or staying with you for years.

As leaders we pride ourselves on the successes of our team members and the loss of someone from the team because they felt unsupported and not empowered to do their job, is always a blow. Everybody knows how this feels from both sides of the coin. Therefore, feedback is the only way to learn.

Understanding feedback

Taking direction is a two-way street. You must be prepared to take this information on board but to also be discerning with the details you are given. The key is to realise that the feedback that is given is always going to be from your boss's perspective. The same if this is coming from the director of a show. The director sees the performance from the audience's perspective and not from the actor's perspective.

Taking direction is a two-way street. You must be prepared to take feedback on board but to also be discerning with the feedback you are given.

I once received feedback from my boss when I was hoping to be considered for a key promotion. I was hoping to hear tangible commentary that would help me be seen in a more positive light within the organisation I was working within. Observations that would help me be seen as the next up and coming leader for the department.

The actual comment was completely unexpected and my response to this was equally unexpected. I remember the conversation well because it was so disturbing to me. I remember thinking, this cannot be real. I remember thinking, how could I be working for such a superficial organisation and if it is such an organisation, do I want to stay?

In retrospect I can laugh about it now, but what I cannot laugh about is what I did on the back of this.

Acting on it

So, what was this feedback I hear you ask?

Well, it wasn't terrible but it was commentary from my leader's perspective which was based on his own experience. It was meant to be helpful and to assist me in my bid for a promotion. Instead, it was soul destroying and left me feeling "less than" when in fact I was completely capable of undertaking the role.

My boss said to me that I would never be considered for the promotion I was hoping for because my hair was too curly. I do have curly hair, but it had never impacted my career progression in the past. He said that the executive team of the organisation saw my curly hair as "crazy" and that I could be seen as "unhinged".

I have to admit that I do have a big personality. This can sometimes come across as overwhelming and sometimes I have been advised to "tone it down a little". I am a performer at heart and having the ability to stand up, with confidence, in front of a large crowd requires a big personality.

However, I had never had comments like this before. It was astonishing and I suspect that it wasn't the only feedback he gave me, but it was the only thing that I remember. I am sure he gave me other tangible ideas but for me, it was this information that stuck with me. How could my hair have a direct impact on my ability to progress in this organisation? If it was a deciding factor then would this be the right organisation for me in the future.

I was distressed by this, and knowing how terrible I was at taking feedback as a teenager, I decided perhaps drastic action was needed, after all a potential promotion was at stake.

I did the only think I could think of.

I had my hair chemically **straightened**!

Now as I reflect back on this action, I am appalled at myself. How could I let such advice drive my action. Something based solely on my appearance. I had been working with the organisation for several years at this point and was mortified that it could all come down to this.

Promotion = Straight Hair

After sitting in the hairdresser's chair for over 3 hours having my hair destroyed, I walked out of the salon with perfectly straight hair. I looked in the mirror and didn't recognise myself. I had allowed well-meaning feedback to completely change me instead of letting it improve me.

I had allowed someone else to take control of me, all for the possibility of a promotion. Every event I attended I felt like someone else. I felt like a fraud. I looked like everybody else; I was no longer me. I kept this straight hair up until someone else was given the promotion and it was at that moment, I realised that if I cannot be my authentic self and be recognised for the value I bring, then perhaps the problem was with the feedback and the organisation and not with me.

Hair straightened – even now it doesn't look like me!

The action I decided to take at that moment was to revert to my glorious curl, stop reaching for recognition in that organisation but to look further afield. Strive for the role I wanted and find an organisation that would embrace my level of "crazy", my curly hair, my big personality and every other attribute I have been advised to change or tone down.

The best response out of this came from my newly appointed executive coach when she said "You need to find your people" and trust me, they are out there. Sometimes it takes a little bit longer to find them but once you have it is glorious.

Be an observational leader

As a leader I am now faced with giving and receiving feedback on a daily basis. Some of it is good and some not so much.

As a leader I am now faced with giving and receiving feedback on a daily basis. Some of it is good and some not so much. The thing to remember is that this is based on your observations as a leader. Be open to what you are witnessing and ensure that you are not making assumptions along the way.

All feedback is useful in a number of ways. It helps you become more resilient if the comment is challenging, it can help you acknowledge what is working and what is not, but for all of its intricacies it will always be useful.

When I provide feedback, I like to acknowledge the good work my team members are doing and if there is a challenging conversation, I like to help them understand ways of improving. I am always mindful that this comes from my perspective and sometimes this can be challenged, therefore when I provide this, I always do so with an open ear. I actively listen and take on board what is being fed back to me.

For someone who inherently disliked feedback for many years I find myself still learning the best ways to provide this. Is it better to rip off the band aid when delivering challenging feedback or to make it more palatable.

For someone who inherently disliked feedback for many years I find myself still learning the best ways to provide this. Is it better to rip off the band aid when delivering challenging feedback or to make it more palatable. I think this depends on the individual. No matter how you deliver it and how you receive it, always remember that there is a human being on the receiving end, either you or your team member. Feedback should be treated with the same level of respect as any other directive.

📝 Key Takeaways:

- *Feedback is a two-way street; you will learn from it whether you are delivering or receiving it.*

- *Feedback should be delivered with respect, as there is always a person at the receiving end of it.*

- *Someone's perspective is not necessarily a call to action.*

- *Practice giving and receiving feedback, this is the only way to learn and improve.*

- *Self-awareness is a necessary attribute as a leader, learn what makes you tick and this will help give considered feedback.*

Cattle Calls and the Brutality of Interviews

Everyone that has auditioned for stage shows knows what a cattle call is. Any audition that casts a wide net will have hundreds of people from all over the country auditioning for their spot. If you are still uncertain, watch television talent shows. The first couple of rounds of these types of shows are known as cattle calls.

You will show up and you will be given less than one minute to impress the panel and win your space in the next round of auditions. Now here is something that you need to understand about cattle calls. These are not solely based on your voice. They are based on everything you present when you walk in the door. Always remember first impressions really do count. You can never make a second "first impression".

In a cattle call, the producers are looking for people with a specific look, specific sound, specific talents that will meet the need of the production that is being performed. The first thing they will look at before you even open your mouth to sing is your head shot. This is the photo you provide before even entering the room.

Sometimes at cattle calls you will not even be given the chance to sing if you do not fit the physical appearance needed for the show. The thing that is most disappointing during this process is that you will generally not be given a reason as to why you have been unsuccessful - you will just be cut.

As I have progressed in my career, I have been to many job interviews. Sometimes just to see what is out there and sometimes because I really want the role.

As I have progressed in my career, I have been to many job interviews. Sometimes just to see what is out there and sometimes because I really want the role. This very example happened to me as I was looking for the next step up in my career. I had been working as a middle manager for quite some time and was unable to punch through to the next level.

I had been coveting the C-suite for a while and this was the next level for me. Just like the cattle calls, there are not as many roles available but far more people applying for them and therefore the interviews are few and far between.

I had been invited to interview for a General Manager IT role and I was extremely excited about it. As I do with all roles, I researched the company, linked with individuals who worked for them and I prepared. The first round was with the recruiter and this went well. Off the strength of that first interview I landed a second interview.

I was provided with feedback to help me on the second round and I attended that interview. It felt good, I linked my transferable skills and addressed all of the questions eloquently. Being well practiced is the key to all interviews (and auditions), never go in cold and try to wing it.

I was then offered the third-round interview. I was getting excited now. This was the role I need to progress my career. I was very excited and felt I would really be able to add value and make a difference in this organisation. It also would provide me with the pathway to CIO and this is what I had been working towards.

I attended the interview and I was well researched and practiced and felt very positive. The interview went better than I had expected. I connected so well with the interview panel that I left feeling that I had the role well in hand. I represented change and the organisation said they wanted change. They wanted what I was offering and I was certain that I had the role.

I waited for days to hear back and as each day went by with no word, I began to feel concerned. I reached out to the recruiter and was told that the organisation was still deliberating but would I be available for a fourth interview if necessary. Well of course I would be available. Were they crazy in asking? This was the role I needed and wanted.

A week went by, then a second week. Surely the deliberations couldn't go on this long, could they? I know what you are thinking as you read this. "She didn't get the job" and you would be right. I got the call mid-week from the recruiter. The organisation decided to go a different way. I was devastated and at that moment thought that I would never get to the C-Suite.

Although I was feeling low, I asked the recruiter for feedback. If I couldn't learn from the experience what was the point of it? The feedback was hard to swallow. I was advised that I wanted too much change and the organisation was not ready for that. How could that be?

They said clearly that they wanted what I had to offer but that was not the case at all.

My learning from this process was simple. Sometimes you think you are aligned with what the organisation is looking for, but sometimes not even they know. When you are clear about the value you bring, you must stay focused on that otherwise you will find yourself in a role that does not meet your needs and you will be miserable in it.

> *Sometimes you think you are aligned with what the organisation is looking for, but sometimes not even they know.*

The lessons I have learned along the way is that you just have to keep on trying. Keep perfecting your craft and building a thick enough skin to weather any feedback. If you want something enough, you have to learn to take feedback, however you need to learn to take what works for you. The hardest thing to do is improve without any feedback at all.

Improvement without comment

When I made the decision to pivot from a singing career into the corporate world, I would apply for jobs and more often than not I would not hear back. I could only approach this in the same way I would approach auditioning. Practice and perfect my resume and cover letter and submit them and by submit, I mean post in the cover letter and resume to the business looking for people. These were days before email, when you couldn't electronically submit it.

Many times, I would not hear back at all. I would send off the documents with all the hope I had and hear nothing. What I wasn't aware of back then was that the organisations were receiving hundreds of responses and, just like with a cattle call, were vetting the applications.

As I struggled to get a look in to the corporate world I so desperately aspired to join, I began to doubt my choices.

They would be looking for key words, elements in the documents that targeted the key aspects of the role that was needed. What I had was a drive for something new but not the exact skills needed to land the job.

As I struggled to get a look in to the corporate world I so desperately aspired to join, I began to doubt my choices. This was prior to reaching out to temping agencies, when I thought my youthful enthusiasm and passion would open the corporate world up for me.

What I soon realised was that any industry, whether it be music or corporate, is hard to break into. You have to show your value, believe in yourself and market yourself. You need to realise that interviews, as with auditions, are a numbers game. The more you audition, the more polished you become. The more polished you become the more confident you appear and this flows into everything you do.

When interviewing, the more confident you appear the more competent you seem. Regardless of whether you have all of the attributes the role requires; your confidence will instil confidence in the

> *When interviewing, the more confident you appear the more competent you seem.*

organisation you are applying for. In reality confidence and competence are two entirely different things and can be seen as mutually exclusive. When singing you have to be both competent and confident.

Without the feedback I desperately needed, I had to find another way of improving. I decided to enlist my closest friends, many of whom were working in the corporate world already. I had reluctantly wanted to share my plans as I had thought that perhaps this pivot might be seen as failure, but as true friends usually are, they completely understood and were more than happy to help.

The support I needed came from my closest friends and they were brutal, in a great way. They helped me prepare my cover letter and update my resume, they helped me prepare for the eventual interview and they helped me every step of the way. Where I was not getting feedback from the corporate sector, I was in fact getting what I needed from the corporate sector in the best way possible from people I trusted who wanted to see me succeed.

Examples of my friends' feedback which I desperately needed to hear:

- Don't pad out your resume with things that are not relevant to the role. Be specific with your examples.

Don't duplicate skills from role to role, state it once, that is enough.

- Think about the real estate of your resume. You only have so much space so use it wisely. Less is definitely more.

- Your cover letter needs to grab attention as does the first page of your resume.

- Highlight your attributes and remember that your resume is just meant to get you in the door. Once you're in then the hard work begins.

- You are not special, everyone applying for this role wants it as much or more than you do, prepare for it.

As I started getting interviews on the back of the resumes and cover letters, I realised that getting my foot in the door was only the first in many steps. Not having enough skills to land roles, I realised I needed other options and this is when the temping option presented itself. One of my closest friends suggested that temping might be easier as the entry point was lower than other roles, and the interview process began.

Interviews go both ways

Just as with an audition you need to prepare, practice and be comfortable in your own skin in readiness for an interview.

In any interview situation you need to be authentic. If you are fun and boisterous then you show a little of that. If you pretend to be something you are not then you may land the role, but will it be the right one for you if you've hidden your true self just to get in the door? How hard will it be to pretend in your new organisation. It's hard to keep that pretence up and will end up being exhausting.

> *If you're afraid to be yourself because you may not land the role then it isn't the right role for you in the first place.*

If you're afraid to be yourself because you may not land the role then it isn't the right role for you in the first place. Remember that an interview is two ways. You are interviewing them as much as they are interviewing you.

A number of years ago I interviewed for a role that I had all the skills for. I was doing the same role in a different organisation and I was looking for an industry change. I prepared for the role and researched the business. I liked the sound of the vision and the company's values and I thought that this would be a good segue in my career.

I had completed the first interview with the incumbent who was moving to a new role within the organisation and they felt I was the perfect fit. They wanted what I had to offer and I was ready for a change. A new organisation presented new learnings regardless of whether the role was similar.

I attended the interview at the offices of the organisation and I really liked what I saw. Then the interview began. Between the two people interviewing me, it became apparent very quickly that this was not the place for me. The individuals on the panel argued with each other. They were not clear about the purpose of the role and did not understand the need for departmental strategy.

Every aspect of the interview made me feel uncomfortable and all I could think of was "how do I escape". I went through the process but could not wait to leave the building. When I left, I immediately called the recruiter and withdrew my interest in proceeding any further.

As I said, interviews are two-way.

Sometimes the job you think you want isn't the right fit for you. Sometimes the organisation isn't the right fit. Just because you have landed an interview does not mean you have to accept the role. It needs to fit you as much as it needs to fit them.

Tips to an awesome interview

When I interviewed for my first temping agency, I explained what I was hoping to achieve. I explained that I was looking for a career change and felt that my transferable skills would enable me to easily transition. I was terribly nervous at this interview and as you can imagine it did not go well.

I interviewed at more temping agencies with nothing to show for it and at the end of the first month, I started to regret my decision. Then something career-changing happened (and you better believe that this went into my career reflection matrix!). I interviewed at another temping agency, and they took me on. What was extraordinary was that the woman interviewing me had seen me perform. What a small world.

She talked about the wedding I performed at. She talked about how well the evening ran, how the music matched the cadence of the event and how wonderful it was. She talked about how happy the guests were and how the evening was simply wonderful.

This was my chance:

- I linked my transferable skills by explaining what it takes to plan a gig.

- The logistics required to sync up the venue, the set list, the equipment and the bride and grooms first dance. Everything needed for making the event wonderful.

- I explained the pressure of getting it right for the wedding. You only have one go at this type of event and if you mess it up, it can be career ending. You can't redo the day!

- I linked the interviewers experience as a customer to how important the voice of the customer is when performing and how this is just as important in the corporate sector.

- What had become a hindrance in all other interviews up until that point became my point of difference.

- We had a common frame of reference and I used this to explain the value I would add.

Every assignment gave me the chance to "audition" for permanency, if that was where I wanted to stay.

From this interview I landed my very first temping assignment. I worked at many different organisations including marketing, importers, essential services, oil and gas, chemical, computers and transport & logistics. All of them very different and each offering me a view into a potential career pathway.

This gave me the experience I lacked to be able to choose the right career path. I was earning a decent living whilst deciding on the career and organisation I would like to have. Every assignment gave me the chance to "audition" for permanency, if that was where I wanted to stay.

Each role was an opportunity to add to my skill set and open up more options on the career buffet and it would not have been possible had I not connected with someone who had seen me perform and I was able to link my transferable skills to my new career path.

Here are the tips I learnt from many years of interviewing:

- **Everything is transferable** – Every skill you learn along your career journey can be transferred to a new role. When you look at a job description look at it through this lens. You may not have exactly what the job adds states but you can transfer a lot of what you have learned into it.

- **Be prepared** – Make sure you do your homework. You want to put your best foot forward but you also want to know about the organisation you may be working for. In the past I have done extensive research on an organisation, reading everything I can about them. Now I link with employees and past employees on social media platforms. This way I can have a conversation and learn what the organisation is really like. Please note that some people may not link with you and feel comfortable providing feedback. Some people may have had a bad experience and the feedback may be tainted. Take it as a data point and use what you learn during the interview process to build your own view.

- **Know your value** – When you are interviewing, it is important to remember that you will be bringing your expertise and experience to the organisation.

Knowing the value you add will improve the interview process for you and the organisation you are interviewing with. You would not be having an interview if you didn't have something that the organisation wants, so don't forget that.

- **Interview them too** – I know that many times I have applied for a role and let the interviewer own the interview. When I was younger, I thought that this was what I was supposed to do. I was putting myself out there and was waiting for someone to "like" me and offer the job. What I realise now, is that I too have a say in my career and where I want to work. I take control of the interview process because I want to know what sort of organisation I am potentially going to be working for. There have been times when I have withdrawn from the interview process because the organisation does not fit my values. This is totally ok.

> *There have been times when I have withdrawn from the interview process because the organisation does not fit my values. This is totally ok.*

Learning from disappointment

For every interview that goes well, you will have stories of the many interviews that do not. Every interview that you left elated only to be disappointed at not landing the role. For every interview there is work that goes into it for the interviewee. You want to show yourself in the best light and the energy taken to prepare can be quite extensive.

What I learnt from the auditioning and interviewing process at an early age was resiliency. When something you believe you want does not go to plan, it can shake you and make you rethink your decisions.

When I was younger, I put a lot of energy into an interview. I would spend endless hours learning as much as I could. As I have gotten older, I still do my research but I also know that the first round is always to learn whether the organisation is the right fit or not. If I think that I can add value to the organisation and learn from the role, then I spend more time preparing for the second round, should I progress.

What I learnt from the auditioning and interviewing process at an early age was resiliency. When something you believe you want does not go to plan, it can shake you and make you rethink your decisions. Every audition was a process of me putting myself out onto public display. Standing in front of people who were judging me. My look, my sound, my movements, everything, would I fit the mould for this show? The one thing you learn during the audition process is that you never really know what is being looked for. You just learn whether you meet it or not.

With every audition and interview there is either elation or disappointment. If it is elation then generally it means you landed it. If it is disappointment, there is also a moment of grief. The energy expelled from preparing and performing (and note that you are performing whether this is an audition or an interview) is exhausting. The grief of not succeeding when you really wanted to needs to be worked through. These things are not fair but they do help to build you up if you acknowledge the grief and learn from the process.

The power comes from acknowledging the sadness and moving on from it. Every outcome can be learnt from. Every decision will lead to another and another and so on. Every delight will have the opposite outcome at different times throughout your career. Everything you experience will help you grow and become more resilient.

Resilience and empathy

Having had so many knock backs in the music industry helped to grow my resilience. From the endless rejections when auditioning I have grown to have a very thick skin. I have often stated that I am incredibly resilient. It takes a lot to knock me down. I am used to constant rejection, which makes me even stronger. My will to succeed and my ambition has been the one consistent factor in my career path.

On the down side, and there is always a down side, I do have lower empathy than most. This doesn't mean I am not empathetic; it just means that I am empathetic to a point. Then I believe you have to pick yourself up and carry on. This level of self-awareness

As I have grown into leadership, I have opened myself up to learning what makes me who I am. I have spent significant time listening to myself and others.

has enabled me to temper my resilience and up the ante on my empathy when needed.

As I have grown into leadership, I have opened myself up to learning what makes me who I am. I have spent significant time listening to myself and others. Understanding that perfection is not necessary if you are passionate and can take others along the journey with you. Resilience is needed but not at the expense of empathy. Human connection is what differentiates us and building strong connections takes empathy.

One thing I learnt long ago when I was singing is sometimes you have to realise that perhaps you are good but not great. Choosing the best path is all you can do and knowing that you are on the best path at the time is being self-aware.

📝 Key Takeaways:

- *Prepare, research the organisation and plan for the interview, make sure it's a place you want to work*

- *Interviewing is a numbers game, the more you do the more proficient you become*

- *Believe in the value you bring, you're interviewing for a reason*

- *Be yourself, you cannot pretend to be someone else*

- *Confidence doesn't necessarily mean competence, but competence can be learned*

- *And most importantly recognise that in every rejection there is a lesson to be learnt.*

Know Your Worth

When I was fifteen all I wanted to do was sing. It was all I thought about, all I dreamt about, all I talked about, until the day that it wasn't. I'd started to become burnt out and my singing career was no longer fulfilling, and just like burnt toast, it wasn't appetizing anymore. Toast smells great until it burns! When the smell permeates your kitchen, it is all you can smell.

You have a choice to make, either eat it or cook something else.

For me this is what happened with singing.

I knew I had a decision to make.

What was I to do?

I had been speaking about singing for so long that I was known for only wanting this dream.

Now I was about to change and all I could do was wonder:

- What would people think?

- Would I be seen as a quitter?

- Would everyone think less of me?

When you make a major change in your life, these are the things that will go through your mind.

All I can say is do not shy away from who you are!

Acknowledge that everyone changes direction, everyone is growing and learning, and change is a part of this.

From someone who prided themselves on preparation, in the singing world, you cannot be good at everything. You have to open yourself up to learning and being honest with what you can and cannot do.

Learning from the mistakes you make and embracing the challenge of change and understanding self-improvement is part of this. Putting your defences to the side and knowing that no matter how old you get there is still so much more to learn and so much more to do.

As I got older and changed my career pathway, my confidence wavered. I was in a different industry, starting at the bottom, having to learn new skills and build my reputation. When I was younger, it seemed so much easier but as I got older, things changed.

Part of my career transition included understanding my self-worth. There were many times when I would accept a role to simply learn something new. I did this in attempt to not feel "less than". From someone who prided themselves on preparation, in the singing world, you cannot be good at everything. You have to open yourself up to learning and being honest with what you can and cannot do.

Eventually I came to recognise what I was really good at and where I needed to improve. The next step was owning it unapologetically and expressing this in a way that would accelerate my career.

Embrace the adventure

As I started to work in the corporate world, I began to notice a pattern. I was good at executing on strategies. In fact, I was very good at coming up with the strategic direction that my departments should be working towards and then delivering upon that strategy.

For me, the strategy became my promise. The promise I was making to my team, the company and ultimately towards shareholders. I had no idea how valuable this skill was when I first embarked on my new found career. I just knew that in order to be successful I needed to be determined in my approach and to provide each of my team with a clear understanding of the direction we needed to travel.

I spent most of my time, initially, observing the departments I would be managing. I would take the time to meet every team member, no matter long it took. I would want to know as much about them as I could in the first instance. I didn't want to make assumptions about my team without really understanding them. Too much of my own corporate career had been filled with assumptions. So much so that I stopped confiding in people about my background.

I became ashamed of my journey when I should have been proud of the strides I had made. I certainly did not want to make anyone else feel less than. The best way to do this, for me, was to spend time with each of my team. I do this even now and I have a very large team indeed.

I would observe the business and other leaders and would take from each of them another piece of the leadership puzzle. The things I thought which would enhance my leadership style and the things I knew I would never do. I wanted to embrace the behaviours of great leadership and dismiss the behaviours that were diametrically opposed to how I saw myself.

Having started from a different base of experience, I always felt less than, however as I began to forge my way in my career,

When you connect honestly with people, they are so much more freely giving of their time.

I realised that by watching others, actively listening and remaining humble I would learn so much more. I found that by truly liking people and wanting to connect made the process of learning so much easier. When you connect honestly with people, they are so much more freely giving of their time. And time is exactly what I needed to improve.

As I grew into leadership, I realised that by being authentic, seeing my work through a lens of joy enabled me to execute on my strategic promise. I started to notice that I was consistently able to do this and my career began to flourish.

Each career pathway that opened itself to me, was more challenging, however I approached the challenge in the same way. Learn, listen and connect. Pave the way forward and design the strategy with joy. Take the team on the journey and empower them to have greater autonomy and to know their worth.

You did it, own it!

As my career began to evolve into the vision that I had, I observed the way my counterparts would own their achievements. I believed that with hard work, I would be rewarded but I noticed that although I was working hard and delivering on my strategy, others were being seen more than I was. I felt that my hard work should speak for itself but I have learned that this is not necessarily the case.

As a senior leader I do find that I sometimes overlook some of the hard work of my team members as I am bombarded by team members who understand the rules of self-promotion. If a leader like me, who has worked extremely hard for advancement in male dominated industries finds it hard to sort the wheat from the chaff, then how can you expect other leaders to do this.

Self-promotion is key to making advancements possible, but I believe that it needs to be done in the right way. For me the only way that self-promotion works is by recognising the people that have made it possible for me to do what it is that I do, and it is also about recognising the hard work I put in to make that possible too.

It is about finding the right balance. Knowing the value you add and how your team are able to take that value and then make it their own. I know my strengths and I know how to make these visible. This is the first step. You can put together your own personal SWOT analysis if you want to understand this more but I like to use my Role & Goal Analysis (see chapter 2). This is where I note my personal value statements.

> *It is about finding the right balance. Knowing the value you add and how your team are able to take that value and then make it their own.*

Being able to define a strategy and then deliver on it is my key strength, demonstrating how I do this is how I own it and promote it. Reporting on the achievements made against the strategy and highlighting the great work performed by my team enables me to share their achievements whilst underpinning my own.

If I have delivered something purely on my own, which is very rare, I will also report upon this and ensure that the value created is clear to my organisation and the executive leadership. Recognising that the value you have delivered is the first step in self-promotion.

There is nothing wrong with stating the facts about the value you have made, just remember that this is seldom a singular activity and to remain true to yourself and honest with your team, you need to ensure you take them on the ride too.

Learn, grow and lead

When I was early in my leadership journey, I had great difficulty in empowering individuals to undertake tasks. I would lean towards micromanaging team members and not give the team the chance to step up. I see this in the young leaders I have in my current leadership team. I think that there is a reluctance to give work to others when you believe that you can either do it better yourself or you don't trust the quality of others.

> *I think that there is a reluctance to give work to others when you believe that you can either do it better yourself or you don't trust the quality of others.*

What I realise now is that in my fear of letting go I found myself getting burnt out and I started to resent my team. This was a direct reflection of my own behaviour, not theirs. I did not understand why I needed to constantly monitor their work. Why the work wasn't getting done and why the quality of what was being delivered was less than expected.

This sat firmly with me as their leader, but back then I wasn't really a leader. I was a manager, and I wasn't allowing my team to grow. As I took on more and more of the work myself, my team became more and more dissatisfied with the work they were doing.

The dissatisfaction grew until I felt that I was failing. The department was under-producing, we were not meeting our key performance indicators and team members started to leave.

I remember thinking to myself "It can't be me, can it?"

It was when one of my mentors advised me that I needed to allow people to make their own mistakes, learn from this and improve by doing. This seemed counter intuitive to me as a young leader. All I could think about was how I would look. If my team made a mistake, then I would look bad. It wasn't about the team at all.

I asked my mentor how I would counter the failure and she said to me "We learn more when we fail than when we don't". She said "To give my team the rope to swing from the trees" and if they falter my job is to prop them up and help them swing from the trees once again.

I learnt more in my first years as a leader by understanding exactly what empowerment was and how if you get it right, you and your team will soar.

Now, as a much more seasoned leader, I lead from the front. I allow my people the room to experience challenges and to grow. I support, actively listen, and let my team fail, learn, and grow in that order. I prop them up and watch them soar from the trees.

If I have learnt anything it has been the strength of empowerment and having the conviction to realise that you cannot do this leadership thing on your own.

If I have learnt anything it has been the strength of empowerment and having the conviction to realise that you cannot do this leadership thing on your own. There is nothing wrong with acknowledging when you slip up, make a mistake or really botch the job.

Trust me when I say this, the mistake you make has been made many other times by all the leaders that came before you. It may not be exactly the same but we have all mucked up in our careers. It is the strength of a great leader to recognise this and to course correct to fix it.

Your leader just wants to know that you are open to learning and improving your skills. This is all we can ask. Learn, grow, lead, become the best leader you can be and know that you are not on your own on this journey.

Key Takeaways:

- *Do not be afraid of promoting your good work. Own it. You did it.*

- *Know your value and continue to improve upon it.*

- *Be self-aware and work towards personal improvement but do not be afraid to show it.*

- *Leaders want to see that you are growing and learning and not afraid to do so.*

Succession

I remember the last performance I sang as I remember the last day in my first job and the last day in all subsequent jobs for that matter. The connection that you make with people is the backbone of anything you will do. There does come a time however, when you will decide that the time has come to exit.

When you perform in stage shows, it is when the run ends. If you are in a band, it is generally when the band breaks up. In the corporate world it will be when you are ready to move on to the next thing. It may be a role somewhere else or career change or even perhaps retirement. The thing to remember is that this is just another transition and will lead onto many other opportunities. Everyone has endings, for without the endings you cannot have new beginnings.

When singing is your career choice, this movement can happen more than you think. Each move to something new is peppered with the joy of learning new songs and taking the lessons you learnt from the previous performance to the next performance.

The one thing that I have learnt from singing and performing is that although a show may come to an end, the things you learnt from other performers are vital in helping to build your skill set. Everything you experience will support you in the next gig. The key is finding the joy in every experience whether it be bad or good. Learn from the things you don't like and adapt them into the things you do like.

> *The key is finding the joy in every experience whether it be bad or good. Learn from the things you don't like and adapt them into the things you do like.*

I remember being in a role in a business I absolutely loved. I knew I was making a difference and I couldn't wait to get to the office every day and do more of it. I worked in that business for over ten years and it seemed to fly past. I learnt, I studied, I connected with team mates, which are friendships and connections I still have to this day until one day when I realised that I had stopped learning.

I had become comfortable and I was stagnant in my role. Don't get me wrong, I still loved the business but I had nowhere to move to. That role would remain the same, year on year, and I started to feel that it was not enough for me.

I knew that the time had come to find something else. The next step, the next platform to grow from. I also knew that there were people that depended on me and I needed to ensure that my team and the business would be well taken care of. For many of my previous roles I had not had the opportunity to prepare a successor but at this business I did.

I made it clear to my manager that I intended to move on and had started to prepare my exit strategy. I had been preparing to leave for quite some time and had put the wheels in motion to build up my successor.

The decision to move on will happen to everyone but the time it takes to find the next role may be longer than you anticipate. Using this time to prepare your successor will leave you in a good place when you eventually resign from your current role. The testament to a good leader is leaving elegantly.

Leaving elegantly

When it is time to move on from your current role you will know it. The reasons will differ from one person to another. For me it has always been when I felt that I had learnt everything I could from the role. Once the songs have lost their shine and have been performed many times its time to move to the next gig.

The thing is to get the timing right and ensure that you have clear successors in place. In the performance space a successor is known as an understudy. This is the person who performs when the primary person is unable to perform, whether through illness or a day off. If you are in a leadership position, you will want to ensure that your understudy is well placed to step in to takeover, whether that be in an interim capacity or full time.

For any understudy the performance is even harder and they have to be even better, after all the audience have come along thinking that they know the star of the show and have paid to see them. When the understudy walks in it is much harder for them. They have no credibility with the audience; therefore, their performance has to be extraordinary. There is a lot of pressure for the understudy.

For the successor to your role, they will be faced with the same credibility concerns that an understudy will have. As a leader in your organisation, you are going to have to work very hard with your understudy to ensure that when you leave the organisation, they are set up for success.

As a leader in your organisation, you are going to have to work very hard with your understudy to ensure that when you leave the organisation, they are set up for success.

Many times, I have seen a successor, who is capable of doing the role they have been supporting, not be given the title, and someone else being brought in. This comes down to the organisation not having visibility as to what the understudy is capable of. If you want to see your successor take the role, you will need to work with them and the organisations leadership prior to leaving to ensure that they are seen as a credible replacement.

Setting your understudy up for success

How many times have you gone to see a stage play or a musical and the understudy is performing. How many times were you disappointed only to be pleasantly surprised at how good the understudy was. You didn't feel like you missed out on anything and you leave the show having had a wonderful experience.

In theatre work, the understudy is generally as good as if not better than the star performer. The difference being the branding of the understudy compared to that of the star. The understudy has a much harder role to play. They have to be excellent every time they perform because the audience have higher expectations of an understudy than they do of the star.

If you want to have some say in who your successor is going to be, when you eventually decide to either stand down or move on to your next role, then there is much work to be done.

This is the same for your successor. If you want to have some say in who your successor is going to be, when you eventually decide to either stand down or move on to your next role, then there is much work to be done.

This work is between you and your understudy and unlike in the performing arts, you really do want your successor to shine. This will come down to the successors personal branding within and outside of the organisation. It will be based upon how credible they come across and how likeable they are in the organisation and with the executive leadership team.

How do you get them there and what are the key attributes they will need to have to succeed you in the organisation? When should you start grooming your successor and when is it time to let go and see how they perform on their own?

To ensure that my successors are given air time I put a plan in place:

- **Mentoring** is a key part of succession planning for me. I ensure that I spend time with those individuals I believe are likely successors. I work with them to understand what they want from their role and help them see the big picture. If they are not interested in my role then perhaps they are not the right person to succeed me. This is important and it will be teased out as part of the mentoring.

- **Multiple successors** are important as each individual will bring different attributes to the role.

- **Branding** will help to show senior management who is capable to take on the role. Everyone needs to be seen and the best way to do this is to have a branding plan in place to bring successors into sight.

- **Hiring** people better than yourself. As soon as you start in role you need to assess the people in your senior leadership team and determine their capability to succeed you. Do this in the first instance as you may need more time to prepare your successors. Hiring individuals who are better than you will free up your time to focus on other tasks and it is easier to build them up to succeed you when the time comes.

By planning for succession, you will provide your organisation with a view of the various attributes they want and who may be best suited to take this on. As with all other aspects of your career, you will need to have succession planning firmly in place. This will differ from the one that your HR department will possibly provide you, as it will include personal branding attributes as well as the various skills that the role will require as listed above.

One way to leave an organisation elegantly is to have some key successors who can easily step in and take over when you leave. This may be in an acting role which eventually may become permanent for the understudy, which is what we all hope for.

Succession planning is as important as career planning and needs to be considered from the time you start in any new role. It is never too late to think about your successors.

Succession planning is as important as career planning and needs to be considered from the time you start in any new role. It is never too late to think about your successors.

📝 Key Takeaways:

- *Don't overstay in a role. Master it and move on.*

- *Get out of the way of your ego, don't be afraid to step aside as you never know what's around the corner.*

- *Everyone leaves, doing it elegantly shows your calibre.*

- *Set others up for success. Prepare your understudy(s) for the role of their life.*

What's Next?

Here I am at the end of my second book, in the coveted C-suite role I had been wanting for over twenty years, wondering what is next? Is it enough to be here or is there something else I want to achieve?

This has always been the eternal question, what is next for me? I have always been incredibly ambitious. I get this from a mother who I believe was born in the wrong decade. She was the strongest, most resilient person I knew but I know she wanted to achieve much more in her career than the 1970's would allow.

Now I have opportunity, a platform, two decades of leadership experience and a network that I am incredibly proud of. Is the next step COO or CEO?

For those of you who have been on the writing journey with me, you will recall the original title of this book. I had intended calling this book "From Singer to CEO" but realised that I couldn't really call it that, having only achieved the CIO title.

As I continued to work through the journey I have been on, I realised that it is so much more than a career pivot from performing arts to the corporate world. It has truly been a journey of career changes, advancement and progression. Sometimes the transitions have been much slower than I would have liked and even now I am perplexed by how slow the corporate world has been in embracing female executives.

I am hopeful that the corporate sector is well on the way to accepting diversity in its many forms within the C-Suite and I eagerly watch as this unfolds globally. I am however, back to the question at hand, what is next for me?

I have always wanted to be the best leader I could be. This has been a driving factor and something I am still working towards. I learn something new every day and as I work with different generations, I find this more and more invigorating, challenging and insightful.

I have a plan (I always have a plan) for the next thing, and perhaps the next book, but I am more interested in your career pivot, dear reader.

I would love to hear how you progress on your career path. Is it turning out to be what you wanted or are you finding yourself having to pivot again? If, for you, it is the latter, I hope that this book will give you the tools to remain resilient in the face of adversity, understand the power of renewal and pivoting into a career that brings you joy and recognising your worth.

From someone who moved from one diametrically opposite career pathway to another, trust me when I say, anything is possible. It will always come down to the planning and execution. Get those two things right and the world will open up to you.

Don't be afraid to pivot, be afraid not to!

And whatever you, **Do Not Straighten Your Hair!**

MB

Appendix

What do you enjoy about the roles you've had?	How do you want to add value and what adds value for you?	What are your non-negotiables in a company?	What are you non-negotiables in a role?
Which companies interest you to work with and why?	What roles interest you to undertake and why?	Where do you see your skills gaps?	How will you fill the skills gaps?

Risk appetite: 1 — 10

$$ appetite: L — H

Fulfilment appetite: 1 — 10

What did you score for your risk appetite?	What did you score for your $$ appetite?	What did you score for your fulfillment appetite?	Analysis
1-4 means you have a low risk appetite	1-4 means you have a low $$ appetite	1-4 means you have a low fulfilment appetite	If you scored low on the risk scale, moderately on the $$ scale and high on the fulfilment scale this shows that you prefer to work in a role that makes you very happy, is a full time secure position that pays within the mid-range bench mark.
5-7 means you have a moderate risk appetite	5-7 means you have a moderate $$ appetite	5-7 means you have a moderate fulfilment appetite	
8-10 means you have a high risk appetite	8-10 means you have a high $$ appetite	8-10 means you have a high fulfilment appetite	If you scored high on the risk scale, high on the $$ scale and low on the fulfilment scale this shows that you prefer to work in a role that has the potential to make a high salary, you are prepared to work hard for little fulfilment other than financial and are prepared to take risks.

SECTION 1: VALUES			
What do you enjoy about the roles you've held?	How do you want to add value and what adds value for you?	What are your non-negotiables in a company?	What are your non-negotiables in a role?

SECTION 2: WHERE TO FROM HERE

Which companies interest you to work with and why?	What roles interest you to undertake and why?	Where do you see your skills gaps?	How will you fill the skills gaps?

Risk appetite

1   10

$$ appetite

L   H

Fulfilment appetite

1   10

SECTION 3: ANALYSIS

What did you score for your Risk Appetite?	What did you score for your $$ Appetite?	What did you score for your Fulfilment Appetite?	Analysis
Risk appetite	$$ appetite	Fulfilment appetite	If you scored low on the risk scale, moderately on the $$ scale and high on the fulfilment scale this shows that you prefer to work in a role that makes you very happy, is a full time secure position that pays within the mid-range bench mark.
1-4 means you have a low risk appetite	1-4 means you have a low $$ appetite	1-4 means you have a low fulfilment appetite	
5-7 means you have a moderate risk appetite	5-7 means you have a moderate $$ appetite	5-7 means you have a moderate fulfilment appetite	If you scored high on the risk scale, high on the $$ scale and low on the fulfilment scale this shows that you prefer to work in a role that has the potential to make a high salary, you are prepared to work hard for little fulfilment other than financial and are prepared to take risks.
8-10 means you have a high risk appetite	8-10 means you have a high $$ appetite	8-10 means you have a high fulfilment appetite